JOHN BULL'S NIGGER

By the same author
NIGGER AT ETON

JOHN BULL'S NIGGER

Dillibe Onyeama

Leslie Frewin of London

© Dillibe Onyeama and Leslie Frewin Publishers Limited, 1974

First published 1974 by
Leslie Frewin Publishers Limited,
Five Goodwin's Court,
Saint Martin's Lane,
London WC2N 4LL

This book is set in 11 point Ehrhardt Semi-Bold

Set by Tinling (1973) Limited
Prescot, Lancs

Printed in Great Britain by Kingprint Limited
Richmond, Surrey

ISBN 0 85632 033 1

To my good friend
JENNIFER THOMAS
*and to black people everywhere
with whom I ask for peace*

The Negro is a beast, but created with articulate speech, and hands, that he may be of service to his master—the White man.
—*Charles Carrol* (Author)

I hate what you say, but will defend to the death your right to say it.
—*Voltaire*

We shall have our manhood. We shall have it or the earth will be levelled by our attempts to gain it.
—*Eldridge Cleaver*
(Black American Author and Militant)

Author's Note

I SHALL BE amazed if this book escapes condemnation for its 'unfair' bias. Granted, I have little good to say herein for my fellow black people. I believe that an author proposing to write an attack should do so all the way and should not yield to the temptation of painting a two-sided picture so as to gain his reader's admiration. I am not blind to the fact that the black man *does* have his merits. I am fully aware of his prowess at games and sports, his sexual virility, and his great talent in art, music and dancing. But these are not new to the world. What do remain unknown are some of the black man's major faults which are largely responsible for his retrogression: faults so serious as to make his merits seem ridiculously insignificant. It is my conviction that until the black man has learnt to overcome these faults, he will remain backward. It is mainly for this reason that I have found no room in my book to delve into his merits.

London, 1974.   Dillibe Onyeama

Contents

Introduction

WHAT I SAY IN THIS BOOK WILL ENRAGE MY fellow black people. This I can understand, because over any dispute involving race and colour the black man will never accept that he has any faults. He always has one and only one scapegoat to answer for his problems—the white man. He himself, however, remains blameless. My chief aim in this book is to show how false this is: to show that the black man deserves little of the considerable sympathy he receives over colour prejudice, and that he himself is mainly to blame for his hardships.

I will no doubt be declared a *persona non grata* by my fellow men, branded the biggest John Bull's nigger in existence, and one of the dirtiest traitors to black people. Terrible though these accusations may sound, I'll risk the labels in the candid hope that what I'm doing may aid my fellow men, inasmuch as I truly believe that a good deal of self-examination and self-criticism would not come amiss in their approach to their lives.

Being black altogether shames me. The general behaviour of my fellow blacks in the world—in particular, those in this country—is the cause for this. It's over three years since I left Eton—in which time I've lived with black people. In *Nigger at Eton*, one of the reasons why I attacked my former schoolmates was because of their disrespect for black people. Well, should my learned contemporaries have followed in my footsteps since I left Eton and shared my experiences among the blacks, they would have hastened back to that famous school with these eager words: 'Listen—about the blacks, you've only heard half the story. Let us tell you the rest. . . .'

To me the black man is more of an animal—only marginally human. My view which concluded *Nigger at Eton* remains unchanged: I'm still convinced that God specially created him to suffer, and suffer he always will. Of course, I could be wrong. I pray that I am wrong. I regret to say, however, that the evidence with which I have been confronted has virtually cast aside any ray of hope that I'm wrong. Only by having his faults exposed can there be any glimmer of chance that the black man could amend his ways and thus refrain from degrading himself and behaving as if he were created to suffer. My sources of evidence will not be confined to my personal experiences since I left Eton. They include retrospective considerations and other people's encounters with blacks.

It becomes serious when a person is ashamed of his own colour. In my case, however, I want to make it perfectly clear that I have no preference for being white. I believe that my shame and the bitter views I've formed against my fellow men would most likely never have arisen if I hadn't come to Britain at the age of eight and remained here so long—thirteen years. African parents are getting rather fond of this method of educating their offspring. Such parents should visit a psychiatrist. Certainly their children should benefit immensely from the superior educational standard of the white man, but these well-meaning parents seem oblivious to the disadvantages of this practice. The outcome of such a practice could, as well as being beneficial, be tragic. The African child emigrating to Britain has, of course, already become aware that the whites are many cuts above his black crowd. He may not know exactly why, but in time he'll discover. Also, of course, he will see stark evidence of the white man's superiority from the far more highly skilled, more highly technological British society that is to govern his life for years and no doubt influence it for the rest of his days. Time passes as he laps up the white man's far richer and more rewarding life. And in his small and slowly maturing mind, his environmental Africa gets relegated to the dustbin, because he has seen the

Britain that is to be his future adventure. As I revealed in *Nigger at Eton*, this was the case with me during my early life in England.

However, they call it 'brainwashing': that forced subjecting of the mind to an ideology or belief of something—something which he, his relations and ancestors had always vehemently rejected. Usually such a kid would be aged between eight and thirteen when he emigrates. Owing to his limited knowledge of life and race, coupled with his curious and naïve nature, he will easily swallow the new ideas the white man dishes out, and for years he'll continue to swallow them. The result is inevitable: a black man with a white mind, or should we say a white man painted black—solely because he was the helpless victim of a thoughtless action by his parents.

The big problem begins when at last he swings (if he does) his lenses towards home. Now the grim task of reintegrating! His attempt to do so will be futile and merely cause a disruptive influence. Having realised that to succeed in life Mother Africa must follow in the white man's footsteps, it's unlikely that he will ever completely fit in with his own people—or ever want to. His only wish now is to assert his position and continue to live and think like the people who led him to lose his identity. The African customs and habits he once loved are now below his standard and dignity. His own people are now inferior to him. He is civilised: they are not. So where does this sympathetic character now stand? Wherever he goes he'll remain an anonymous nigger. His name is Immigrant in Britain, Nigger in America, Bantu in South Africa, Aborigine in Australia, and when he turns to his fellow black men it will be John Bull's. The whites naturally can't accept him as one of them: he is the wrong colour. His own people certainly wouldn't tolerate him as he is now. So rejected in both worlds, he has an extremely hard struggle within himself in no-man's-land.

As time presses on, the tension tightens as he battles with his desolation and predicament—till the day when he inquires with deep solemnity of himself: 'Who do I really belong to?' It's difficult to see any hope of a turning point. The acceptance of being wholly black again is out of the question. The thought of being a bit 'backwards' once more is too discomforting and hard to bear. The reality of the white man's superiority over his people is so stark in him that there is a psychological defeat which inhibits him from striving to overcome that barrier that the white man has so strongly fortified in his mind. To make the most of his unfortunate position would appear to be his only solution.

You'll probably think that exactly the same predicament would confront a white child brought up in Africa in the same way. I personally have never met or heard of a white person being brainwashed by Africans. Should that happen it must definitely be assumed that his brainwashing would be temporary or transitory, for, as he grows older, he will see where his white brothers hold the balance of power. Inevitably, he will take sides—naturally, with his white brothers.

Now, allow your minds to travel into profound contemplation. Consider the gravity of one losing one's own natural identity. You have to conclude that the best word to describe such a sad affair could be nothing but TRAGIC. Imagine the shock that confronts the parents and loved ones of the anglicised African lad after his return home. He may well be the learned gentleman they were expecting. But was losing his identity among their wishes for him? What would otherwise have been joy and happiness on their part that he is well-educated is substituted by pain and staggering disbelief that as a result he is virtually ashamed of his race and colour. Let's pray that at this point they'll come face to face with reality: that they were the un-witting cause of this tragedy. Such a tragic anticlimax wouldn't have arisen had they waited till their child reached late teens at least before packing him off. At that age one assumes that he's too African to be brainwashed. That is true from the point of view of his age. He's old enough to think for himself. He has enough sense to question the validity of the white man's ideas rather than accept them with a blind eye. Brainwashing can only arise if it's a deliberate policy on his part to be brainwashed: if he has firmly decided to spit on his own natural way of life and assume a false identity. The choice is entirely his own. He's fully aware of the course of action he is taking and is solely to blame should he suffer as a result. He has voluntarily chosen to be brainwashed, while the poor child has had it forced upon him like some undersized sweater on a fat boy. In London (where I've lived so far) I have only come across a few cases of the former but a good number of the latter, and both casually and in depth discussed with them the question of brainwashing. The majority of the latter, though their brainwashing ranged to different degrees, had two serious factors in common—a nasty friction between them and their parents, and a rather poor relationship with their fellow blacks in England. None, however, struck me as being ashamed of his race or colour. Most of them had plans to return to their motherland for good, though all acknowledged that to reintegrate fully would be one great battle to be won. Of the few who were uncertain about returning home was a girl in her late teens, whose brainwashing case was more dramatic than the other African youths I met. She was a gregarious girl who seemed to have 'graduated' in hemp-smoking and had taken her place among the hippie groups. She had lived in this country over half her life—sent by her parents to study. Her parents have now disowned her. So badly had the English white-washed her brain, she and her parents were no longer on the same wavelength. It reached a stage when the frustration of being isolated in a world of her own crammed her head with ideas of suicide. Fortunately, her hippie allies talked her out of it. However, she had no wish to remain in England—a country she didn't belong to; but even more, she couldn't dream of returning home, with the stark knowledge that to rediscover her lost identity would mean a long, torturous search. This she wasn't yet ready to face.

In most ways I'm in the same boat as my fellow brainwashed youths. My mind is virtually a hundred per cent white. As a result my attempts to mix with fellow blacks in London have continually produced electrifying results. Likewise the case with my parents. Since my seventeenth birthday we've totally failed to see eye to eye on so many different matters. My holiday breaks in Holland frequently contained fiery disputes and rows. So tense was the atmosphere in our house for those four years that you could slice it with a knife. One matter we usually conflicted over was my view that the black man was an animal. Much as they found my views very distasteful, they believed them to be the juvenile thoughts of a young, rather brainwashed child. They used to say this. They reckoned that by the age of twenty, I should be mature and reasonable enough to dismiss such childish thoughts. I always disagreed. And sure enough—by twenty, my matured mind had firmly and decidedly retained its belief about the black man, grinding my parents' hopes to dust. Thus, seeing that I had a closed mind, they abandoned all efforts to advise, reprimand and argue with me. For years they had tried and had totally failed. As I had now virtually reached manhood, it was too late to persist. I continued to express my racial views and they put up little contest. They were no longer concerned about my thoughts and beliefs. And it was with mutual satisfaction that on 6th January 1972, my twenty-first birthday, they washed their hands of me. I was my own master as from then. My future was my affair.

Had I always heeded their words, thus effecting a good relationship between us, they would be supporting me still. My only evidence for this statement is my thirty-year-old brother's case. He was supported till he was twenty-five. BUT he didn't come to study in this country till the age of twenty and passed from a Nigerian public school to Guy's Hospital, London University. He has always been in my parents' good books—*because* he came to England at the correct sort of age. Brainwashing in his case was not really possible. Many, many Africans have passed (and still do) from African secondary schools to British and other Western Universities. My old man himself didn't leave for Britain until he reached late teens. This is all clear-cut evidence that Africa offers sufficiently good education to pass her students to Western Universities. What then is the great necessity for parents to send children off to Britain? Is it really worth it? Doesn't it do them more harm than good? ... Some serious re-examination by African parents into their action would be of importance; otherwise, as in the case of my parents and others, the open arms of regret and disappointment will most willingly embrace them.

Though I acknowledge brainwashing to be a nasty affair, I confess that unlike other victims of it, I experience delight and pride at having been brainwashed. Foolish though Africans may be for sending their children to Europe, I express my warmest thanks to my old man for having done so with me. During the few years leading to my twentieth birthday, my thinking machine had been at full throttle in trying to solve this question: was I mad and abnormal to think the way I did of my fellow men and to be ashamed of my colour? All the while I was fully conscious of my state of mind, and I have to confess that I used to experience a vague sense of disgrace and discontent at being so frightfully brainwashed. But by and by these feelings faded away, because, the idea took definite shape in my mind that my being brainwashed to such an alarming degree was the best thing that could have happened to me. To start with, I realised that as a result I was in the ideal position to assume the role of judge and jury (and I did so) as regards the furore and severe tension that had existed between the black and white races in the world. Here I was—a black African and victim of two cultures: born into one and shovelled into the other like coal into furnace; impregnated with the ideas of the people of both cultures for an almost equal number of years. It can thus be correctly assumed that as a result I possessed two mentalities. Much as I was white-minded in normal, everyday life, I had by no means lost touch with the black man's approach to thinking problems. I could still consider and view matters in the same light, appreciating and understanding them as he would. So, equipped with two contrasting viewpoints, I imagined I was qualified to set myself up in judgment over the bitter racial unrest. And in addition to that reason, I had had the benefit of a good education.

When I was twenty, I started to scrutinise the racial problems in our midst. I realised that at that age I was virtually a man. I imagined I was above average intelligence. I was old enough to trust my own thinking and judgment, and I did. Until then I had only viewed the tension between the two races from the white man's angle. Having been brought up to see the whites as being basically superior to my fellow men, I had always accepted the former's arguments and ignored the latter's complaints. So at the age of twenty I started seriously to ponder over the racial palaver with a completely open and unbiased mind. Was the black man really an animal? Was I justified in seeing him as

that? Who was really responsible for his blunders and hardships? Himself? The white man? . . . I rationalised my thoughts,
winnowed them, summed them, and reached the sad but irresistible conclusion that, all in all, my fellow men were the
criminals. I concluded also that I was justified in seeing them as
animals. And as I have stated, my feelings today are unchanged.

Soon I began to experience the stated delight and pride at
being brainwashed. I realised that if, being black myself, I positively saw my fellow blacks as animals, it was surely a great
advantage for me. Why, wasn't I then in a position to volunteer
some concrete suggestions as to how they could improve themselves? . . . I wasn't so naïve as really to believe that Dillibe
Onyeama's own special criticisms and suggestions would bring
about a vast change over the black peoples' attitude to life. But
I knew that my attacks were valid and I could volunteer some
concrete advice.

Yes, brainwashing was the best thing that could have happened
to me. But for its occurrence I would never have come to see my
fellow black man for the animal he is. Why, I may well have
turned out like him. I would never have dreamt that he was
mainly at fault for the racial palaver in this country, and I
would never have realised the need for some severe criticisms.

Before I proceed, this is as good a moment as any to explain
whom exactly I refer to when I say 'the black man'. Much as
the whites refer to all people with dark skins as 'black', I, in
fact, only see those from Africa, America and the Caribbean as
such: only people of African origin in the world. But my attacks
will be confined to the Africans and the Caribs (better known as
the West Indians) in this country and in Africa. Much as my
knowledge about the Afro-Americans is limited, I am, at least,
very much aware that they are the *only* blacks in the world
worthy of any sympathy, with more than enough cause for com-

plaint against the whites. We've all witnessed the never ending hardships they've suffered at the hands of the white Americans, and their bitterness at the ill-treatment towards them, I fancy, accounts for their serious attitude to life—unlike their fellow men outside America. Knowing they are brothers, and fully appreciative of their plight, they realise that to keep together, an effort to maintain solidarity is essential, and that they do. With their race riots and creation of active societies such as Black Power, Black Panther and Black Muslim, they've left the world in no doubt about their sincerity. They are thoughtful over their future and have shown their determination to progress at all costs and gain equality with the whites. They have made a firm resolution to show that they too are human beings. As the black American militant Eldridge Cleaver says in his book *Soul on Ice*: 'We shall have our manhood. We shall have it or the earth will be levelled by our attempts to gain it.'

In the case of the Africans and West Indians, however, we have a completely different story. We see the Devil's disciples. We see the biggest bunch of hypocrites alive. We see a group of people so unbelievably aimless, callous and abstract: a group of people who thrive in causing their own hardships and taking the easy way out by directing the blame to the white man. We see a group of people who are successfully proving that they are anything but human beings.

So there we are: in America the good nigger suffers under the white man, and in the rest of the world the wicked one is the main cause of his own grievances. Either way, it seems, the black man suffers. That's why I'm convinced that he is born to suffer. Then there's the information in the Bible about Ham, the son of Noah, and forefather of the black race. Owing to his discovery of Noah's nakedness, Noah's wrathful reaction was a prophecy against Canaan, Ham's son: 'Cursed be Canaan; a slave of slaves shall he be to his brethren'—meaning that Canaan's black descendants were doomed to be the down-trodden of the earth. However legendary it may sound, however stupid it may seem to use such an example, we have to admit that in view of the black man's bitter hardships throughout the years, this curse has so far been fulfilled. This explains why I attach so much importance to it. It would appear then that the black man's suffering is based on a sacred truth. So it would seem that by proceeding with this book I am banking on the hope and fantasy that the black man is not necessarily born to suffer and that we may see an end to his hardships. You will naturally conclude that if my fellow men are doomed to be tormented, then any question of there existing a stable relation-ship between them and the whites becomes farcical. Well, even assuming that my people are not conceived for suffering, the possibility of general harmony ever developing between them and the whites is still as unlikely as harmony between a mon-goose and a snake. I have discovered that it's impossible. My reasons will unwind themselves in the course of the book.

1

I BEGIN BY RELATING THE STORY OF TWO
black men who were toiling on a cotton plantation. One was
called Sambo, the other Lambo. The torturous afternoon sun
was threatening to burn them three shades blacker, and they
sure did sweat. Presently, Sambo stood up and wiped the pers-
piration off his forehead. Next moment he was gaping in paralysed disbelief. There, on the edge of the plantation, was a white
man—leaning against a tree, drinking beer. Sambo swung a
belligerent face towards his partner. He boomed, 'How come dat
white trash yonder 'im drinkin' beer while we is sweatin' here?'

Lambo stood up and looked. Rage like that of discovered
treason flared in his eyes. 'Man, dat goddam sonnofa white
bitch!' he stormed. 'Ah'll be damned!'

'Ah got somethin' to ask you, honkie!' Sambo snapped, then
marched off to settle his score. Arriving at the tree, he eyed the
white man as sweetly as a vulture eyes a carcass and asked
sharply, 'How come you is drinkin' while we is sweatin' to hell
out there?'

With an air of cool authority the white man replied quietly,
'It's a matter of superior intelligence, Nigger.'

'Now what de hell you mean by dat?' Sambo snarled.

The white man smiled. 'I'll show you, Nigger.' He stepped
aside, held out his hand flat against the tree, then challenged the
scowling Sambo. 'Now let's just see how hard you can punch my
hand.'

Sambo's eyes bulged. He grinned. It was that big, famous Louis Armstrong-like grin: a grin full of stupidity and emptiness such as only a black man could give. He swung a mighty blow at the hand. The white man calmly removed it at the last moment, and Sambo's fist slammed the tree with all the force of Hades. As he danced and bellowed in anguish with pain, the white man resumed drinking with an air of smug unconcern.

'You see, Nigger,' he said, 'it's a matter of superior intelligence. You didn't reckon I was really going to let you break my hand, did you?'

Pain-stricken and humiliated, Sambo returned to his partner.

'Well,' rasped Lambo, 'what de white trash 'ave to say?'

'Man, dat cotton-pickin' honkie!' Sambo seethed. ' 'E say is a matter of superior intelligence!'

Lambo gulped. 'What de hell he mean ba dat?'

Sambo quickly glanced around him—no tree. One moment of quick thought, and he had it! He grinned ecstatically at Lambo and nodded.

'Ah'll show you what 'e mean, Lambo,' he said, bracing himself. Then, placing the back of his hand against his own forehead, said, 'Lessee how hard you can whup ma hand.'

You've probably heard that one before. It's fiction, of course. I'm more painfully conscious of it than any other racial joke—for one reason: it's so incredibly realistic. Let me hear it now for the first time with the characters' names and colour concealed, and I would connect Sambo's actions with a black man. They are so characteristic of a black man. I could never picture a white person in such a situation. In the mists of memory I seem to recollect somewhat similar incidents actually taking place during my youth in Africa. To me it's of great significance, that joke; for it serves as a brilliant, clear-cut example of what the black

man is—positively stupid! And one of the worst aspects of blackness which causes me great shame to be that colour is that the
black man, as a whole, has not yet captured the art of reasoning
and fails to use that God-gifted phenomenon, thought. That big,
empty grin is always there.

Since I left Eton, one of the causes of my great headaches
about the blacks has been their very presence in Britain alone.
And here is an assortment of examples of their failure to think.
As is well known, of the profusion of West Indian and African
immigrants who have voluntarily crowded Britain—mostly
West Indians—the vast majority, I'm sorry to say, are here for
a new life. And the ones that return to their motherlands to do
some good—normally African students—are, comparatively,
very few indeed. In the case of those here to stay, we know that
it's only the much better pay and living conditions that attract
them. Till this day I've remained resentful that they are so
blinded with the materialistic gains of monetary returns, that
the vast majority gladly occupy positions which the bulk of the
whites consider below their dignity to touch. Occupations such
as porters, street-cleaners, railway-men, bus drivers and conduc-
tors seem to be the main attractions. I'm not talented enough to
describe the feeling of humiliation and disgust that has surged
through my body as I daily witnessed these existing situations.
The immigrants have clearly failed to see the image of the black
race they give the whites: that they are only equipped to perform the most menial and base work. In their case these tasks
are degrading; because when the whites turn away from such
unpleasant but essential social services *in their own country*, it
becomes the height of disgrace that the blacks should abandon
their motherlands and hasten to occupy these rejected positions
like dogs taking bones from their masters' plates. The blacks
perform these tasks as if it were right and proper for them to do

so: as if they were specially created for such a display. In black countries it's black people who see to the menial social services. It's the duty of the whites to do likewise in Britain. I've failed to see why it must be blacks.

Often I've argued with white opponents of Enoch Powell over the reasons for their opposition to the repatriation of black immigrants. Their reasons infuriated me. 'God! If the immigrants went the whole bloody country would come to a standstill! ... Who'd run our buses and undergrounds? ... Our streets would become filthy! ... Our hospitals would be seriously handicapped! ... We need the blacks ...' On the profusion of occasions on which I've heard these statements, my white opponents spoke in normal tones, as if revealing a universal truth. So the image the whites have of the blacks is crystal clear. What torments my senses above all is that the blacks seem only too willing to fulfil that image. It's not, therefore, so much the whites who are insulting the blacks by promoting this image, but the blacks insulting themselves. I never tried to hide my emotions from my white opponents when they made those remarks. So far, I've been successful in making every one of them see my argument and fully appreciate my reasons for ardently supporting Enoch Powell.

Many of the black immigrants have obtained enough qualifications to get better jobs at home than they have here. Though the payment here is much higher, the same applies to the cost of living. In the long run, therefore, things would even out. Instead of returning they prefer to attempt to reach the level of the whites by trying to settle here rather than return home to a level upon which they can all manage, irrespective of the fact that to settle and manage with the whites has proved difficult and disruptive.

One reason some have volunteered not to return home is

that their countries have nothing worthwhile to offer them. Fair enough. But my one question to that is quite simply: why can't they return home and do something about it?—Go back and make their homes more attractive and habitable? . . . The painful truth of the matter is that the black man is minus any spirit of self-sacrifice and devotion. All that swims around in his mind are vivid pictures of himself as the proud owner of some neat-looking house; pictures of himself settled in a comfortable sitting-room with his family, gazing with glee at a new television set; sitting coolly and commandingly behind the wheel of some wretched motor-car. Luxuries like these are the black man's only desire. That he should have them now —today—is essential. This is the mentality of black people. It amazes me that they really believe Rome was built in a day. God knows that the luxuries of Western technology were not the result of some magical incantation. The whites of yesterday all the while planned ahead. They applied considerable research and hard work to their ideas: in addition, patience, sincerity, devotion and the will and determination to improve themselves. It took time, but today the white world triumphs. My fellow men fail to grasp that owing to their handicap in technology, brought about by their different cultural circumstances, the question of their reaching the white man's standard today in any quick time becomes ludicrous. To reach that stage will require that very patience, hard work and self-sacrifice that the whites successfully employed to build up their societies. The blacks don't have the stomach for this. In truth, they care damn all for their countries: their only interest is to share and enjoy other people's dinners rather than prepare their own. My finger points at the West Indians, for instance, and I ask you to consider how many of them searching for a new life in England have thought about the future generations of their people? Has the thought of overlooking the stated luxuries, returning home and trying to raise and develop their motherland for the enjoyment of their descendants ever crossed their minds? This to them would be unheard of. Let the West Indies fester on. Let their descendants learn the hard way. Every man for himself. Enjoy what there is now. I'm sorry to have to confess that this callous attitude is part of the black man's nature.

I will always admire the services of the late Albert Schweitzer, the Swiss mission doctor, in Gabon, West Africa. He was white. Voluntarily, he went to Gabon and built his renowned hospital at Lambarene: built it in eternally steaming jungle with his own hands and African help, operating far into the night under the most primitive conditions. For many years he continued his long fight against leprosy, sleeping-sickness and a host of tropical diseases, in surroundings of famine, pestilence and floods. Later, thirty white doctors and nurses went to help him.

Out of sheer humanity, white people sacrificed themselves for the sake of the Africans' welfare. This throws a very shameful light on the black immigrants' absence of concern towards the welfare of their fellow men. Unattractive their countries may well be. But we must then remember the location of Dr Schweitzer's hospital and seriously ask ourselves: 'Where could be more deadly and unattractive a place to go and inhabit than the African jungle?' Yet, unconcerned about the risks facing them, Schweitzer and his thirty aides proceeded. It was a question of hard work, patience and confidence—and the road to success was finally reached. What would have seemed an impossible task was conquered. If the West Indians in this country returned home in large numbers and laboured in the same way as Schweitzer, new, healthy and beautiful West

Indies could surely emerge out of the ash and debris that it is now.

One important factor we should observe about the black immigrants is that many are dishonest over the reason for their presence in England. Rarely will you meet one who will summon the courage to admit that the immigrants swarm over here only because of that basic myth in the black man's mentality that the streets of London are paved with gold. Look at the celebrated Speakers' Corner, for instance: the boisterous cosmopolitan ground in West London's Marble Arch adjoining colossal Hyde Park, where a great influx of tourists swarms during summer weekends, to observe and listen to speakers rave on about politics, race and religion. Black orators are in the majority, and are also the most bitter. *The white man* is the constant target of their fury. Sweating profusely, they stand on boxes gesticulating wildly with obscenities and accusations bursting from their lips like staccato blasts of submachine-gun fire. Often indignant white members of their audience storm in defensive protest: 'Why are you bloody well living and working in a white man's country then? Why not go home?'

'Ah, but you see, I don't work,' comes the crafty answer. Then a very smooth and smug explanation: 'I live on social security. I sleep with your women. Every week I wake up in the morning and collect my dole, then I take a stroll in the afternoon. I've got nothing to contribute to your country whatsoever. I've simply come to exploit you like you once came to exploit me.'

I've heard this sort of reply from black people more times than I can possibly remember. They are convinced that by being here they're giving the whites a taste of their own medicine. I've come across many expressing grim delight at the fury shown by Enoch Powell and his supporters at the over-whelming number of immigrants coming here, the reason being that the whites wouldn't leave Africa on the initial request of the Africans. I've failed to understand the blacks' refusal to realise that both in Africa and in England the white man has been the boss. He has indeed had the very best of both worlds, and the black immigrants' idea that they are exploiting him in return becomes ludicrous. They use this talk of exploitation merely as a means of expressing their bitterness against the whites and their lack of interest in any amicable relationship with them. A great chip rests on their shoulders for the oppression they've suffered from the whites in the past and present. Having now settled in this country, the return of this oppression in whatever way possible seems to be their only interest towards any relationship with the whites. Exploitation was a part of this oppression. I've often wondered what stupidity this is. Why are the blacks incapable of being realistic for a change? It's disturbing that the filth from the streets of London has soiled their brains to the extent that they're unable to realise that by performing menial tasks in England, *they* are being *further* exploited.

The blacks who subsist on social security may well feel happy and smug at the comforting thought that by being paid for nothing, they're retaliating against the white colonists for depriving them of their minerals and raw materials. But I have these candid questions to ask them: Is this truly the standard of living that they are happy to maintain for the rest of their days? Don't they have the least intention to improve themselves in some way? . . . Certainly the amount made from social security couldn't possibly be compared with the astronomical value of the minerals and raw materials which the whites took from Africa—not to mention that these natural resources were of no use or value to the Africans, and lay untouched in the soil like stones. The blacks seem to overlook the fact that they don't command the social security system nor draw money at will. The white man finances them voluntarily. He has the power of give and take, and again I stress—he holds the whip! So, to dismiss these fantasies of counter-exploitation would not be detrimental to the black man's thinking machine.

If the blacks had sufficient vision, not only should they perceive the absurdity and falsehood of their stated utterances, but also that it's the height of foolishness to make challenges at Speakers' Corner or anywhere else. Many years ago they would probably have been stoned for this slur. Yet in their own countries today they would surely be stoned. They fully recognise that the vast majority of them have nothing to offer besides their unskilled labour. They are aware, too, that as a result of their voluntary crowding into Britain they are not exactly welcome, since the widespread belief is that they are the chief cause of the alarming number of unemployed here. Yet, in the midst of the problems and hostility they've created, rather than quietly proceed with their business and if anything—remain obscure—many, with a total lack of *thought*, exhibit themselves and provoke further enmity with offensive challenges. And they're the very people needed to create the basis for a viable society. The British government would surely be doing them a great favour by repatriating them. At home they would be compelled to work for a living.

The stated example of aggravation by them of the whites may seem petty. Here's a much more serious one.... It is evening at Speakers' Corner. The sun is just disappearing over the horizon. The crowd is slowly diminishing. Almost everybody's attention is hooked by one of the few remaining speakers. He's a middle-aged, thickset African of smart appearance which, however, is counterbalanced by his grotesque ugliness. Like some God of Wrath, he screams: ' . . . Kill all the whites!

I tell you we must all get together and kill all the white bastards! The only good whites are dead ones!...' The bellows of encouragement and delight from the black members of his massive audience are mingled with a roar of fury and protest from the whites. Some enraged white person summons the police. About eight arrive. An Inspector makes his way to the speaker. A devastating silence falls upon the crowd. The roar of thick traffic in the background is unheard at that moment of excitement. The Inspector grimly confronts the speaker. In the firm legal manner that befits his calling, he orders him to alight from the box, for his speeches are inciting racial hatred. Never should he make such statements again! The speaker stubbornly refuses to come down and announces that this is Speakers' Corner, where one is free to say *anything*. The Inspector counters that *inciting to kill* is illegal *anywhere*. Five minutes of severe wrangling, then the Inspector warns: 'If you don't come down, I'll have no option but to arrest you.' An explosion of booing and abuse erupts from the black sympathisers, who close in menacingly on the Inspector. 'Produce a warrant!' cries the speaker in defiance. 'You'll never take me without a warrant!' A thunderous roar of support from the blacks. 'Not if we can help it!' from a few is answered by cheers of agreement. The Inspector looks uneasy and uncertain as to what to do next. A slight pause. Then, decidedly: 'I'll give you five minutes to get down or I'll have to make an arrest.' He turns and is booed through the crowd by the blacks. The speaker, completely unmoved, continues his bitter tongue-lashes. The Inspector and his colleagues look on helplessly in anger. Five minutes pass. Ten. Twenty. They do nothing. An hour later the speaker voluntarily gets down. Applauding 'black brothers' crowd and escort him from the park. The day is won.

I watched that incident in silence. I remained convinced that

the only reason the police failed to act was out of fear of causing a racial punch-up. I personally felt it inevitable had they
taken action. The following Sunday was a carbon copy of the
first. The same man uttered the same incitements, this time
with two Inspectors asking him in vain to stop it, pointing out
that this was punishable by imprisonment. The third week
told the same story—until at last a firm advice from fellow
blacks made this thick-skinned speaker see reality. He was
overdoing it, they told him sharply as he left the park later. He
had made his point, so pack it up! Also, it was the height of
stupidity to be screaming 'kill the whites' with police Inspectors
present as witnesses. I agreed with that last point.

Regarding such deliberate and unjustified acts of provocation,
I've often been led to wonder how the white man has continued
to tolerate the blacks within the midst of his culture. I've
seriously questioned the amount of truth that exists in the
belief held by blacks in England that the colour of their skins is
the only reason why the English hate them. I won't for one
moment try and deny that the whites hate the blacks. But I
ask: why? Basically, owing to the colour of their skins? Or
could it be that the whites have been *aggravated* to the extent
that all they could show to black people is nothing but hatred?
. . . I believe the answer to be more of the latter. I feel that the
amount of hate the blacks hold for the whites doesn't compare
with that which the blacks themselves have caused the whites
to hold for them. I'm further convinced that should the whites
arrive at the point of having to openly unleash their hatred,
we would witness a bloody race war, and there's no doubt in
my mind that my fellow men would come out second best. But
no. There's the harsh Race Relations Act to prohibit people
from being overt with their prejudices; there's the Institute of
Race Relations to promote closer contact between the races;

and there's the Race Relations Board to investigate and settle complaints of discrimination. Yet every day black people complain that no one pays attention to their views. As I see it, the white man in England has tried to cure that disease called racialism: tried to bring about harmony between the black and white races; and my fellow men have done nothing except hamper the white man's efforts. They should consider themselves very lucky. The whites have exercised such tolerance towards them that it it is difficult to believe. Only when the torturous screams of people like the black Americans ring in our ears can we find room for pity in our hearts; for we know that little is being done by the white Americans to stop colour prejudice or bring closer relations between the two races. But what do my fellow men here weep about? The white man has stooped down enough on their behalf. What more do they want? . . . As I explained earlier, it all basically stems from the white man's long history of discrimination against them, especially the agony they suffered in the slave-days. Their bitterness was further inflamed by the birth of Enoch Powell's racial speeches in the mid-1960s. And, since then, as the thick-skinned politician persisted with his speeches, pitchforking the racial tension to alarming proportions, the black peoples' grudge against the whites has simply reached its zenith, with hypersensitivity to go with it. Should they be involved in any trivial conflict with white people, they would instinctively believe there were undertones of colour prejudice. I could relate many events involving blacks and whites which could not possibly have been associated with colour; but the blacks wanted to believe (and did believe) that it was all prejudice against their colour.

To illustrate this, I once met a very pleasant lady in her late 'fifties. Very respectable, she was proud and self-conscious of being English. This harmless lady clearly had no race bias of any sort—particularly as she was fiercely opposed to Enoch Powell. Yet one day, she had this unfortunate experience. . . . She climbed on to a bus with her small dog. No sooner was she seated than she was rudely challenged by the loud-mouthed black conductress who created a scene by announcing that dogs weren't allowed on the bus. The passenger was surprised for she had often taken her dog on buses without any confrontation. An argument arose, during which the conductress lost her temper and shouted: 'Don't look at me like that just because I have a black face!'

If that examole of hypersensitivity is one you could classify as being absurd, here's another one. . . . At Speakers' Corner, one evening, a group of black people were on about immigration. Presently, a young constable approached from a distance. On reaching them he stopped, and as politely as one could expect, asked that they start preparing to leave as the park was due to be locked up shortly. For this harmless request he was met with blatant protests from the blacks, who barracked him and indignantly asked why he should inform *them* of all people. Why not approach one of the *white* groups? . . . Quite taken aback by this sudden outcry, the policeman assured them that he proposed to inform others. The blacks' insolent retorts were that they knew when the gates closed: he didn't need to tell them, and they had no intention of being hurried. Calmly, the policeman explained that he was only doing his duty by reminding them. The blacks reluctantly accepted that and turned their backs on him. He quietly went on his way, leaving them to spout racial obscenities among themselves.

Again I watched in silence. My sympathy was with the policeman. He had not shown any feeling of offence or ill-will, and was performing his duty. It just happened that blacks were the first group he came across on his route. I saw it as being merely another opportunity when the resentful blacks craved to show their hate for the British police, who, they are convinced, victimise them because of their colour.

So, thanks to the activities of Enoch Powell, my fellow men suffer from hypersensitivity. Powell is at present the main bug in their minds. He bears the stamp of a "racialist" simply because out of all immigrants in Britain the non-whites have been the target of his craving for repatriation. What a narrow-minded assumption! Nobody can positively prove whether he is or is not colour prejudiced. The fact that his speeches have been directed against the non-white immigrants doesn't necessarily mean he is. His basic aim is to point out the dangers of immigration before the situation reaches chaos. One must admit that in a country being swarmed by aliens, an enraged citizen of that country dying to see a halt and some repatriation moves would fix his eyes on the race of immigrants whose number is outstanding as compared with the rest, and constantly snap at them. This is human nature. One would naturally find it discomforting to know that one's *own home* is also to be inhabited by an alarming number of aliens, coupled with the knowledge that this would inevitably create a grave dilemma in accommodation, employment and the country's economy. Certainly, I would hate it. If the Chinese were the most populous among an incessant stream of multi-racial immigrants pouring into my country, I would, in my anxiety, be prejudiced against the Chinese for that one reason—their presence in such abundance: not because nature produced slat-eyed, yellow beings the size of runts. Whichever race it may be—be their colour white, yellow, red or even blacks from another country—I would express my prejudice against any of them. Furthermore, should I be in a position to make my feelings heard, that I would do! And there

38

could only be one method of ensuring that my views might make any headway—by speaking the same kind of inflammatory language as Enoch Powell. I remember that in one of his racial speeches he created a major storm by referring to 'grinning piccaninnies'. I'm convinced that this wasn't because he hated blacks for their colour, but to make his feelings about their abundance here really felt by the masses.

If I haven't in the slightest cooled down my fellow men's bitterness with my reasoning, then I'll try it further with examples that will surely show that Powell's hollering for their departure is not necessarily because of their colour. An almost parallel example to the British immigration problem was that of Ghana, in West Africa. The only difference was that she actually ordered all unauthorised aliens to leave the country by December 1969. Her chief and continuing headache were the Nigerian immigrants (fellow black Africans), as their population in Ghana was excessive and was far higher than that of any of the other numerous alien races. The Nigerians specifically were ordered out. So should we accuse Ghana of being racialist?

Then, there was Nigeria herself. This time there is an 'internal immigration' problem. As was evident from the civil war, there had been long-standing enmity between the Hausas of the north and the Ibos of the east. This was because over a million Ibos were living in the north, employed in the key positions. With the Hausas vainly agitating for their departure, it reached the stage in 1960 when, furious at what seemed imminently like their domination, the Hausas not only drove the Ibos out of the north, but massacred 33,000 of them, carrying out the most inhuman tortures. And in due course, during a political debate in the north, an Hausa politician made this statement: 'The Ibos belong in the east, the Hausas in the north, the

39

Yorubas in the west, and Lagos (the capital) is a place for all! This was met with great applause. It meant that everybody had a home of his own to live in. Doesn't that apply to the black immigrants in Britain?

I think it's abundantly clear that when one's own home is faced with too many immigrants, for one to lash out at the most populous section of them is only natural and is not a question of their actual race or colour. It so happens that the most crowded immigrants in Britain are dark-skinned people. With regard to my two examples, my fellow men must admit that Britain has exercised a lot of patience towards them. Their repatriation has only been *suggested*. Yet any black country confronted with Britain's dilemma wouldn't merely stop at suggestions. As a further example, in 1968, East Africa actually began expulsion of Asian citizens who wouldn't take up national citizenship and at the same time wished to continue living there. Of a total population of 21,000,000 people in East Africa, the Asians numbered a staggering 600,000!, and were the most populous of over a million aliens. So my fellow men here cannot be complaining at Britain's so called 'prejudicial' attitude when their own countries would proceed several steps further.

It's unfortunate that the history of colour prejudice has been long, agonising and never-ending, causing the people of today to be very colour conscious. For that reason one can't say a word to the black man without risking an accusation of colour prejudice—even if there could not possibly be any question of colour and the matter could apply to anybody. In view of this, Britain deserves some sympathy over her dilemma with the dark-skinned immigrants. And that dilemma isn't only confined to their growing population. Naturally, Powell is also concerned at the signals black people give out. He has obviously seen them for the very touchy and self-centred characters they are: characters bearing a grudge against the whites, seeking some sort of vengeance, and totally lacking the desire for any amicable relationship with them. Powell is therefore justified to fear a race war in his own home. He couldn't have rammed home the point to the masses in better words than his provocative, 'I seem to see the River Tiber foaming with much blood!' His anxiety to see the back of my troublesome fellow men can well be understood.

My fellow men jump to conclusions too quickly. They should learn to analyse a matter with meticulous care before making a hue and cry. If and when they do learn, they might realise that such a matter could well have a completely different interpretation to what they had initially believed. Maybe they would accept, for instance, that Powell isn't necessarily colour prejudiced. They could, at the same time, cast aside their popular belief that Britain is governed by racists simply because Powell has not been imprisoned and has been permitted to remain in Parliament and press on with his speeches—with apparent total disregard for his expulsion from the Shadow Cabinet.

Certainly, there are some whites in England who are basically colour prejudiced. But then this is natural. I won't try to be a philosopher by making a moral exploration of the reasons behind colour prejudice. Briefly, there are all sorts of reasons why people in the world hate each other, and *race* hatred is one. Anywhere in the world some will discriminate against you for your race, tribe or colour of your skin. It stems from hate, which, by right, is a vital aspect of human nature. But my fellow men won't take this into consideration. They are only obsessed with white people who are colour prejudiced, completely overlooking the fact that there are sympathetic ones who do put in some efforts for their happiness.

The time has come for my fellow men to appreciate that life isn't just a bowl of cherries. That their ancestors experienced hell in the slave days doesn't automatically mean that life today must be heaven for them. It seems to me that this is what they expect from Britain. The fruit of life will always have its sour tastes; and I'm afraid to say that my fellow men's attempt to accuse the whole of Britain of being colour prejudiced for every petty conflict they encounter is unjustified particularly as she does condescend to be tolerant and sympathetic towards them. My fellow men merely take all this for granted. They regard it as being right and proper, as it makes up for the atrocities the whites committed in the slave days. If they stopped to think, they would see that their constant outcry over those atrocities is now much ado about nothing. The matter is past and finished, and nothing more can be done about it. The whites don't try to deny their criminal record. They'll acknowledge their guilt and admit that they acted despicably against the blacks. What more can they do but condemn and regret their crimes?

I'll end the matter with that question. My principal aim has been to open up this book with a pedestrian glance at the chief and immediate issue over race in Britain—namely immigration by dark-skinned people. This is where one of the blacks' greatest defects—their inability to reason and think—is outstanding. If only they could, they would surely realise that their very presence here—being exploited—is just not fitting. They would realise that while in a country reluctantly suffering the agony of their high population, yet being tolerant and seeking methods of effecting a good relationship with them, it's sheer idiocy to purposely try and provoke hostility in return on invalid grounds. They would recognise, too, that the actual colour of their skin is of little importance to most people, and it's all really a question of hypersensitivity on their part. And, in conclusion, they would also see that the suggestion of their repatriation isn't only justified but also a brilliant one; because their motherlands are crying out for them.

2

WHY, OH WHY, IS IT THAT THE WHITE MAN USES that faculty of thinking and the black man fails to do so? . . . Day in and day out my mind tussles with this question. Every minute of my life I'm fully conscious that I've travelled from one dilemma to another. First, cruel colour prejudice at Eton, now the shattering disillusionment of discovering that my contemporaries' opinion of my fellow men was so painfully correct —black and therefore stupid! I have to bear the dilemma of being black and suffering the bad name my fellow men in the world bring upon us with their atrocious behaviour. Every day I stare at black faces in the streets, in buses and in trains. I become engulfed in bewildered contemplation as I scrutinise the thick lips, the wide, flaring nostrils and general negroid features. I can't understand it. The intensity of that word is sketched in bold strokes on every line of their faces—stupid! They genuinely look as stupid as their actions seem to suggest. Perhaps it's my imagination. Perhaps frustration at their thoughtless actions has overwhelmed me to the extent that subconsciously I crave to believe that they look naturally stupid. Perhaps I need to question my sanity. I don't know what it is. All I know is that my feeling towards my fellow men is fast becoming one of detestation. During moments of frustration, I've candidly wished that those in England could be rounded up into a reserve and shipped off home.

To illustrate the sort of behaviour that places me in this state of mind, I was at Waterloo main line station one morning to meet a close relation of mine arriving for his half-term break from school. I **waited** outside the platform, taking in the sights and sounds around me—till one particular spectacle caught my attention. Some thirty yards away was a casually-attired black man with a child around five or six years of age. And, under the very noses of the passers-by, he unbuttoned the boy's trousers and allowed him to urinate on the ground—and there was a 'GENTS' only nearby. Then, to add the final touch, the man looked around him and exposed one enormous grin. I turned colder than an Eskimo's nose, my face aflame with shame and disgust. Quietly, I looked on, not failing to notice the offensive expressions that clearly marked the faces of some of the passers-by. The questions raced through my mind like a silent film: could this brainless fool not appreciate the sense of what was indecent and indiscreet? Could he honestly not sense the wrong in this? What also rankled was that grin. What was its purpose? To justify his action? I've never found an answer to that question.

This is the sort of action that causes white people to have a very dim view of us. Clearly, that man gave no thought to the possible impression gathered by the bystanders. Either that or he was unconcerned. And, who knows, he may well belong to the bandwagon of blacks who always grumble that the whites hold them in little regard.

Following that incident, my memory has constantly drifted back to that evening a year or two back when I watched a television programme on race relations. At that time, my home was an international mixed hostel in West London's Bayswater, and I saw the film in the spacious television room with other students. Blacks and whites were interviewed separately, being allowed to voice their views and complaints against one another.

46

I've never forgotten one particular English lady, among whose bold complaints was one that black women allowed their kids to soil the pavements. I well remember that the black students watching the programme were fuming and loudly called the woman a liar. I myself attached little importance to the programme at the time and drew no conclusions. The incident at Waterloo, however, proved that woman's point. Nor was it an isolated case. On a number of occasions in due course my eyes have had to endure the torture of witnessing black women allow their kids to soil the streets of London. My immediate reaction was to hasten my steps, feeling ashamed to the very guts. What has rankled most is that I've never seen any member of a non-black race performing this act—just blacks!

One repulsive habit of so many black people which I'll never get used to is their spitting in public: their loud clearing of the throat and spitting. They do this in the streets and from their passing cars in utter oblivion. I know some white working-class folks do the same, but compared to the number of blacks with the similar habit, the former are very few indeed. Such an action is characteristically black. When my thoughts turn back to my early days in Africa, I remember that it was a common habit among the folks and knew virtually no class barrier. On many of the occasions when I came across blacks doing this in London, I had to fight to hold back the outrage my throat begged to roar. Why they can't show a little more discretion is something I fail to understand. Fair enough, at home it's considered a petty matter. But surely common sense should tell them that in a white country where the folks have different moral standards and will judge you by your actions, such a thing is neither done nor appreciated. But common sense, it seems, is the one thing too many black people lack. Time and time again I've sat on buses and in tube trains and listened to blacks clear their throats for the world to hear.

Yes, it's true that the whites in the world have a low image of us. It's true they view us with much ridicule and amusement. They do so with my blessing; because they are so justified. God knows that people don't form ideas of others on hypothetical grounds. They are given cause to. The blacks in the world have presented the white man with enough causes to promote certain images of them. And, furthermore, my fellow men have the knack of fulfilling every image the white man has of them, yet at the same time bawl that these images are false.

Take, for instance, that controversial British show *The Black and White Minstrels*. I'll begin by relating a dispute about it in my family. It occurred in Holland in 1968, during the Christmas holidays following my final departure from Eton. Being on rather bad terms with my parents at that time, I offered no viewpoint: just listened silently. It was in the elegant sitting-room one night, and present were my old man, my senior brother, myself and two younger brothers—all comfortably lounging in armchairs and on sofas. The programme on television was the *Minstrel Show*. We viewed in silence—till the face of a black minstrel was displayed in close-up for some seconds. The silence was then interrupted by my thirteen-year-old brother—the younger of the two—suddenly blurting out, 'Gosh! I must say he looks just like a black man!' That cracked the whip! He was instantly jumped upon by my old man and my senior brother. Quietly, though forcefully, they forbade that he ever repeat that. The black minstrel, they explained, with his feigned black face and white lips parted in a mock grin, was the image the whites had of a black man's countenance: a false and abusive image that was vehemently disliked by black

48

people. And here was my brother, they added, virtually acknowledging that this was his natural expression. My younger
brother, a clever and highly argumentative little devil, was
very amused at their outburst and questioned the offence
caused by the show, as it was merely an entertainment. His
opponents attributed his inability to see the offence to his
young age. My elder brother pointed to the television and
explained firmly: 'That, my friend, is just making a mockery
of black culture! Why project black man's culture through
whites when there are so many blacks in the world available to
add reality to the show?' My old man agreed. My younger
brother fully appreciated the reason but sheepishly insisted
that if the black minstrel resembled a black person in his eyes,
he should be free to say so. My old man amusedly granted
him that point but denied him the right to say so within his
hearing. My brother carried on a futile argument from
there.

For some unearthly reason, never, until listening to that
dispute, had I been aware that the *Minstrel Show* was regarded
with contempt by my fellow men. I personally had never seen
anything remotely offensive in it. And till today I still don't.
I've always felt that the black minstrels portray an unquestionably realistic image of my fellow men. Now and again I've come
across complaining black people voicing the same points as
my old man and my senior brother in that dispute. I've totally
failed to see how they could regard the black minstrel as being
a false and abusive image of us. As is well known, our obsession
for music and dancing, compared with that of the whites, is as
good as abnormal. And of the exuberant varieties of music,
the most popular are lively rhythms. Owing to my fellow
men's physical state while dancing to such rhythms, an image
of us is projected through the *Minstrel Show*. As their limbs

fly out in all directions like india-rubber, simultaneously, eyes roll like spin-discs, and thick lips expose an enormous array of white teeth as the frenzied dancers grin like a hunk of water-melon, uttering guttural sounds of glee. And where it's mere singing alone, you'll still find the black man's expression being similar to that of the late and renowned Louis Armstrong: ablaze with an ecstatic grin.

When I view all this from the white man's eyes, I can fully appreciate the humour involved. Clowns, as it happens, are very popular jesters at circuses and pantomimes in white countries; and it so happens that the general state of my fellow men while dancing, particularly their facial expression, is extremely clownish. It surely can't be said that the whites regard it comical in the ridiculous sense, but just plain amusing and entertaining. They do appreciate it immensely. Obviously they decided that the contrasting facial expressions in dancing between the black and white races would make a splendid flavour for an entertainment such as *The Black and White Minstrel Show*. And the only way to ensure that the amusement of the black facial expression was fully brought out was, quite rightly, to make as good an imitation of one as possible. To have genuine black minstrels would, if anything, make the show unrealistic. Because my fellow men, presented with a totally different rhythm of music from their own, surely would not, or could not, dance to it as they do at home. The two would not be compatible. Thus, the vital fun of the facial expression—which, in truth, has been the passport to success for the *Minstrel Show* —would not be sufficiently displayed—if at all.

My fellow men don't view the matter from the whites' angle: only from their own. That's why they're compelled to believe that the *Minstrel Show* is aimed at making a mockery of them. Certainly the actual basic resemblance of a black minstrel's face to that of a natural black man is very poor. In that sense one can classify it as being false. But in imitating genuine black expression, the black minstrel thoroughly succeeds, and it's surely an undeniable fact.

I can't understand why my fellow men allow themselves to be disturbed by such a petty matter as the *Minstrel Show* anyway. Even assuming that the whites are intending to make a mockery of us, so what? As long as my fellow men are proud of their culture, the white man's attitude shouldn't matter to them. The white must retain the right to present their own shows as it best suits them. The truth is, firstly, that black people have a shockingly low sense of humour as compared to the whites, and will receive the most harmless jests directed at them in bad part. Secondly, they see the facial expressions of the black minstrel and the other famous image of them—the gollywog —as being ugly. This makes them believe that the whites regard black people as being ugly. I myself haven't shown much interest in these images, though I do find their facial expressions amusing. But I do believe that they betray the white man's thoughts of black facial appearance as being ugly, which doesn't worry me at all. I remember that on the occasions when I expressed my amusement at these images, my fellow men were always contemptuous, dismissing me as another brainwashed nigger. It was the same with racial jokes—which I adore immensely. On numerous occasions when I cracked jokes about blacks when in their company, I usually found myself laughing alone. Jolly embarrassing, I must say. Heads would shake sadly, followed by words like: 'I feel sorry for you. The white man has really played havoc with your brain.' They angrily dismissed my criticism that they were hypersensitive and should learn to laugh for a change: jokes were not meant to be injurious but good fun. They always countered that the white man only meant them harm in everything he did or said concerning blacks.

I'll never cease to remind myself that if my fellow men offered the brains in their heads as much attention as they do to the white man's emotional attitude towards them they would be a million times better off. It serves them right that the whites regard them as being ugly. Before I forge ahead with explanations, let me say that regarding the question of my fellow men's physical state while dancing, I'm very proud of black music and dancing, and am completely at home with such aspects of black culture. I'll always admire the physical state of the musicians and dancers—as this is a natural manifestation of black music when performed for its own sake. There can be no question of my finding their expression comical in itself: it simply causes me to feel a greater sense of appreciation and delight for the music and dancing. I only become averse to that expression when my fellow men are merely making caricatures of themselves for the white man's amusement. That is to say that such facial expression isn't confined to when they dance and sing. In other circumstances it has been a source of headache for me to the extent that I regard it as obscene and animal. My fellow men complain that the black minstrel and gollywog make them out to be ugly. Yet it is well known that they are always ready to be exploited in the most sickening manner on the screen to fulfil these images. Sporting their famous servant roles, watch them expose vulgar apish grins, contort their faces in all sorts of revolting apish ways, open those thick lips as widely as a basket and emit disgusting apish sounds and laughter. Watch them go out of their way to look like the 'grinning piccaninnies' and 'watermelon men' that they've been so suitably nicknamed by the whites. Yet when the whites inevitably laugh, shower us with nicknames, create unfavourable but realistic images of us, my fellow men are resentful. Having frequently sat in cinemas and watched such outrageous displays, I've always felt sick at the pit of my stomach.

It's equally discomforting when I have to witness the same facial expressions in real life—this time caused by black people's volcanic mouths. To be more explicit, their voices must be heard above everybody else's. And all I can do is suffer the embarrassment. I well remember the reaction of a young black relation of mine to the din of a group of Africans in a small West End African restaurant. 'Honestly, we blacks! Why must we always be so noisy? Just look at them. They look so ugly!' He watched for some moments longer then sighed with disgust and said: 'Really, we are animals, aren't we?' I was forced to agree.

On another occasion an English brunette was my guest for dinner there. A few other white diners were present. My guest and I couldn't hear ourselves speak as we ate, because of the noisy conversation of three Africans at the next table. Presently, my guest whispered with irritation in my ear; 'Why can't they talk quietly? Why do they make so much bloody noise?' From the depths of my humiliation I could only reply: 'God knows, honey.'

Whenever I go into the presence of black people, their loud mouths have always got on my nerves—in the streets, on buses, shops, pubs, everywhere. Those lips furiously flap, escorted with the bulging of eyes; the uproarious laughs sound like hyenas when uttered by women, like baboons in the case of men: nonetheless, in both cases, virtually every part of the interior of their mouths is visible. In *Soledad Brother*, the celebrated book of Afro-American George Jackson's prison letters, he put this question to his mother: 'Have you any theories why

53

blacks talk so much and so loud? A Chinaman told me once that blacks were the oldest and finest people on earth "but one thing wrong, talkie—talkie—talkie . . ." '

My only explanation as to why blacks are so loud-mouthed is that such was how nature produced them—comparatively, very noisy people indeed. Back at home in my African environment or in any other black country, I would think little of the matter. Because my fellow men would then be in their own natural environment, living as they were naturally created. Here in England, a white country, I find it very off-putting. White people, generally, are quiet and want a peaceful life. Noise caused by scientific creations alone has been a source of illness for them. Noisy people won't help the situation. And of course, the gesticulations and facial expressions that black people display to decorate their constantly flapping lips will surely be regarded as ugly in the eyes of the whites, and, I imagine, also contribute in supplying the food for bad images of us.

You have to agree that one would show more respect for a quiet person than for a loud mouth. There's something curiously suggestive about a quiet person. He has the atmosphere of a peaceful being, respectable, gentlemanly and possibly bright and clever. A loud mouth, however, stocks one's mind with discouraging ideas—a troublemaker, perhaps. That's how I compare the whites with my fellow men. With the average white man one observes a casual smile: he chats in normal, quiet tones: one observes a general calmness and self-control about him—a human being indeed. Whereas, with the average black man, his loud mouth, his wide-eyed gesticulations and laughter and his enormous grins, seem to me to suggest stupidity, incompetence and wildness—very animal.

Noise is one of the great dilemmas you're faced with when

you live with a black man. Apart from his loud mouth, his
record-player, for instance, will blare almost every day to the
point where your attempt to concentrate on something would
be quite impossible. Irritation sends you marching to his room.
Somehow, you control your annoyance enough to be polite in
your request for less noise. But bet your bottom dollar that
you'll not even receive a casual apology. He'll meet your
request, but that cynical tone of reluctance and incivility in his
agreement would be unmistakable. You thank him and return
to your room, only to discover that there is only little subsid-
ence in the noise, but out of tact you won't repeat your visit.
You're keen to avoid a row, because you know that he'll most
likely react emotionally. This is the black man. Noise being a
fairly outstanding aspect of his nature, there isn't the least
consideration on his part that as he drowns the house with
noise some poor soul somewhere might be plagued by it.
When he's politely asked to tone it down, he feels insulted.

Since leaving Eton, I've lived in three different houses with
black people, and this has been my experience with them all
along. However, I've forced myself to get used to their noisy
ways, knowing that if I'm to reintegrate fully I must begin by
accepting my fellow men as they are. So, in the absence of white
people, I usually remain undisturbed by the black man's
clamorous habits. In addition, I find I can ease off my hard
feelings at the fact that nature had to select us to be the noisy
ones. BUT, let my fellow men display their noisy habits in
public or in the presence of any white person, and my hackles
rise. Because since I regard the whites as basically superior
to my fellow men, should the occasion arise when their contrasting moral standards are exhibited together, I instinctively become white-minded. I recollect a scene where a fat
black woman behaved in a way that was reminiscent of mothers

in my African environment. The matter took place in a 'black' area—South East London's Lewisham (where I lived for over a year)—outside a row of shops on a quiet lane of semi-detached houses.

The quietness of the morning was disturbed by the bawling of a small child some four years of age. His mother lost control of her temper and set to delivering him the most brutal slaps around the head, shouting her fury as she did so. 'Brutal' is the word I use, and I seek to pronounce it with a capital B. She knocked the poor child down, throwing him into frightful hysteria. Shocked passers-by watched and exclaimed. A few gently tried to beg for mercy. The stiff-necked black woman merely departed, roughly pulling the child behind her. Had I been a passer-by, God knows that I would have been too ashamed to stand around. As it happened, I was waiting my turn for service in the newspaper shop—silently boiling with humiliation. Service of the few customers was slightly delayed, since the scene caught our attention. I felt very uncomfortable when the stout lady behind the counter eyed me of all people as she remarked: 'Oooooohh, that was a bit harsh.' While the others expressed their agreement, I offered no reply. Of course she would look at me in particular, just because it was a black person guilty of the brutal act and I was the only other black present. Brutal, that is, in the eyes of white people. As I explained in *Nigger at Eton*, that form of punishment was commonplace in Nigeria. To black people it was trivial.

It seems that the world must know of all my fellow men's actions and utterances. I remember that in one area of Lewisham I had to get used to walking along the pavement in full hearing of black people's laughter inside their homes; mothers scolding kids, and husbands quarrelling with wives. From the pavement almost every word or detail of the goings-on

56

was audible. Since my fellow men are so obsessed with the white man's emotional attitude towards them, they would earn some respect from the whites if they could curb their noisy habits for a start.

In view of all this, I've seriously wondered why my fellow men have encountered prejudice from white people in accommodation. It has been the subject of much controversy over the last few years, this question of prejudice in accommodation. I think that the whites are fully justified in being averse to housing and living with my fellow men. I've discovered that my fellow men's chief problem isn't that their skin is black, but because of the way in which they behave as tenants. Understandably, in the eyes of the whites, some of their natural habits are animal —noise being a perfect example. A noisy person, as I said, has the air of a troublemaker. That's what you risk when you let a black-skinned tenant through your front door—trouble; and it will leave an indelible scar of bitterness and regret on your memory. Should I ever own a house in England or any other white country, black people could only become my tenants over my dead body. Waiving their noisy habits, they are usually dirty and untidy tenants. I've visited many black homes, and this has applied in most of them. Visit the bathroom and toilet, for example. Instantly, you will grimace. The room sobs, miserable and uncared for. The eroding wall-paintings are damp and dirty. The floor and lavatory are much worse, littered with matches and cigarette butts, etc. Then, there's the kitchen. Again the walls suffer from dirt, dampness and cracks. The sink, grey with filth, is probably filled with grimy water containing cutlery, crockery and cooking utensils merely dumped there till their owner feels like washing them. There's no consideration on his part that somebody else may wish to wash-up. The floor is unswept. Food and litter of all sorts surround the litter-box simply because apathetic characters couldn't be bothered to ensure that litter is put inside the bin—that is, that the bin should not be over-filled, as is usually the case. And, of course, there's an unpleasant smell to go with the unsightly spectacle. All this is enough to show you that somebody still needs to learn how to live. This is the black man in England. By black standards this way of living may be acceptable. But to white people it is not. The sooner my fellow men appreciate this, the better—that is if they expect to be put up by white landlords—and tolerated by white tenants. I used to know a very quiet and affectionate American girl of twenty-five who was on a year's visit to England. Her first home was a West London house owned by a West Indian. She was the only white tenant among six blacks including the landlord. She had stayed there barely two weeks than she was craving to move out. It took her three weeks to find suitable accommodation: and during her search she had been particularly anxious to avoid another black house. She had really been disgusted by the first one. She complained that the atmosphere was extremely tense between the tenants: they were frequently quarrelling, and several times fighting broke out between them. The landlord was uninterested and never bothered to intervene. What repulsed this girl most was the filth of the place. 'It was so dirty!' she stressed through clenched teeth; 'the kitchen and bathroom especially. Nobody ever bothered to clean the place.'

My personal feeling towards my fellow men's standard of living has been one of repulsion. I have considered myself lucky that I've not had to live in some of the filthy black homes I have seen, because I wouldn't have survived in any of them. Only one of the three houses I've lived in with black people has been positively foul—that being the one from which I write now, a depressing four-storey building in South-East London.

I've been here now for seven months; and though I swear every day that I'll move out soon, I have no plans to do so. Somehow, I'm managing to tame myself. I've been striving to escape from the grip of snobbery that was the result of my Eton education: trying to teach myself that even though I went to Eton, I must learn to make do with the conditions facing me, however appalling they may be. My presence here *still* suggests that I am making do.

I remember my landlord's wife once telling me that she would never accommodate white tenants, as they were bound to run off saying that black people lived filthily. Out of tact I held back an opinion that was in my mind. Such white tenants surely wouldn't say that unless there was some truth in it. And if the landlady knew jolly well that she kept a perfectly clean and tidy house, she wouldn't be afraid to accommodate white people. In truth, the landlady knew her house was dirty, and that was why she was against putting up white tenants. The house is worse than the typical black house I've already described. For three months now the bath has been out of order without hot water, and though I have on several occasions informed the landlord and his wife, nothing has been done about it. The bathroom-toilet is usually like an animal's cage. The floor is perpetually damp, and litter of all sorts 'decorates' it. Rubber tubs containing the stinking laundry of the other black tenants are carelessly dumped on the floor and in the bath. The basin is hardly ever washed after use, and the same applied to the bath when there used to be hot water. Regularly, I've walked in there to find that somebody has urinated on the floor around the lavatory seat and also on the seat itself: what's more that the lavatory has not been flushed after use. One of the rooms near mine usually stinks like a cowshed; and to add to this torture is the fact that the three people who share it have the knack of leaving the door open—exposing a very untidy room and the sickening sights of pots containing urine. I have always closed the door and flushed Air Freshener on the landing to kill the odour.

In addition to these major drawbacks, somebody took out the bulbs on my landing and in the toilet; and for two weeks other tenants and I had to find our way in the dark. I never thought of buying new bulbs myself, as I saw that as being the landlady's duty. I mentioned it to her one day as I was telling her about the bath, only to be angrily shouted at and told that I was much too fussy: that if I didn't like the house I should quit: otherwise stop bothering her. Not wishing to inflame her further, I said nothing. I wasn't particularly angry at her indifference as I knew it to be only too typical of black landlords. So long as they get their rent, their tenants can go to hell as far as they care. Consideration for their tenants' comfort is something they lack completely. As it was evident that my landlady had no intention of buying those bulbs, I did so myself.

Often I've invited white girls to my bed-sitter; and on all of such occasions I've rushed up the stairs in front of them to make sure that the door to that foul-smelling room was closed. Then, later on I've sent up quick prayers to God that my guests wouldn't request the use of the toilet—owing to its usual shocking state. Sometimes God fails to answer my pleas: they do ask for the toilet and my heart sinks. I can't bear to imagine what thoughts (if any) they would form about us blacks should the bathroom be in the usual dirty state. In fact, on a number of occasions, no sooner had I made my guests feel at home than I excused myself and left the room. Like a bat out of hell I thundered downstairs to the bathroom to ensure that the floor, sink and toilet were immaculate, and the room generally presentable. If not (as has usually been the case), I took control of the situation myself, uttering foul-mouthed curses against anyone who should arrive and most considerately defile the place once more.

On the occasions on which I walked with white friends towards my home in South-East London, I was constantly aware that I was taking my guests to a black area: conscious that I was an old Etonian living in such an area. I felt ill-at-ease, in case my guests should be wondering how an Eton man could be at home in such unattractive, third-class district rather than somewhere like that snobbish region, Park Lane. My memory has often flicked back to two different occasions in Lewisham when I met white girls who actually expressed their surprise that an Etonian was living in such a place as Lewisham. Hiding my awkward feeling, I agreed, but explained that I was trying to reintegrate with my fellow men. Nowadays, each time I have a white visitor, I'm tempted to bring up the question of the area I'm living in, giving my reasons for being here. I merely want to get the matter out of my system: want to redeem myself for failing to live in the sort of region that was expected of Eton products.

Yes, constantly I remind myself that I'm living in a black area, and as a result, I suffer from acute depression. Yet at the same time I'm fully aware that I wouldn't fancy the idea of moving into a 'posh' white area, because though I am white-minded, my colour is not white, and never in a million years could I think of myself as a white man. I would never really be happy in a completely white area. The spirit of isolation would haunt me, as well as one of guilt that I was abandoning my own people. God knows that if my fellow men lived as gracefully as most whites, I'd be only too proud to live in black areas. As it is, all that most black people show is a dirty existence.

I've visited most areas of London with a high black population. I can't describe my feeling of discomfort as my eyes take in the signs of imminent squalor that scar the surroundings in virtually all the black districts. Everything is grey, unsightly and highly depressing. Even when the streets are well swept it makes no difference: an unsavoury greyness hangs over the whole district all the same, in particular, with the slimy-looking houses. And to heighten my discomfort more, the loud mouths of grinning black figures, spitting here and there. As I walk silently along, I feel an atmosphere of foreboding and of impending doom. This, I have up till now gravely interpreted as meaning that in the not too distant future, most of Britain will be truly foul and unpleasant to inhabit, and black people will mainly be the cause of it.

3

NOISE AND UNCLEANLINESS AREN'T THE ONLY factors that place my fellow men in white people's bad books. There is another major factor—violence. Comparatively, the black man is a very violent person indeed. Violence is as important to him as a wing to a plane. Without a wing a plane can't fly. Similarly, without violence a black man can't function. Violence is much more a black 'language' than a white one. Whereas the average white man would use the faculty of reasoning to settle a dispute, the average black man would, in preference, resort to violence. In addition, he is highly sensitive and quick-tempered as compared with the white man. Words are the easiest weapons to use in hurting him. However polite your intentions may be, if he doesn't like your words, his skin is painfully pierced. Make a simple request for less noise; oppose him in an argument; or criticise him, and the likelihood is that he will react emotionally and become aggressive. As for criticising him, you would be inviting a blow on the chin. It would be as good as abuse, and abuse in one thing that rankles the black man intensely.

It may interest one to know that owing to my fellow men's aggressive nature, white people aren't alone in being prejudiced against housing them. They are accompanied by *black* landlords! I've only met six of such landlords; but through them I learnt that many other black landlords found their fellow men frightfully troublesome tenants and were averse to housing them. Apparently, the troubles start when the landlords approach tenants to take up necessary matters regarding the house. Rather than listen and accept quietly, tenants feel insulted at being ordered. Instantly they argue, raise hell and are ready to fight.

One of the six landlords was a thirty-year-old, bull-necked West Indian named John; a cheerful 'good-time' guy. He was painting the stairs in his semi-detached house one day, having pinned a notice downstairs warning his tenants to be careful not to tread on the painted parts. One young black tenant came downstairs and did just that. John was naturally furious and screamed his rage. All hell was let loose then, for the tenant hated being shouted at, became defiant and lost his temper. Next moment he drew a flick-knife from his pocket and threatened to kill John if he uttered one more word. Tension and fear kept John's mouth tightly shut. He stood there helplessly as the incensed tenant swore obscenities at him, then went out of the house. John went to the police station to report the matter, but apparently the officer told him: 'I'm sorry, Sir, but we can't really do anything about it until he actually cuts you.' Which made John just as bitter towards the police as he was towards the tenant. 'Suppose he cuts me and kills me?' he complained angrily. 'Fucking cops!' Anyway, in due course he threw that tenant out.

This was just one of several of his experiences with bellicose black tenants. He and the five other black landlords I mentioned vowed that never again would they accommodate black tenants. They were sick to death of their pugilistic tendencies. They believed that black people were to blame for the prejudice they encountered from white landlords—solely because of their troublesome nature, and not so much because of their colour. The black landlords themselves were prejudiced against white people, but for once found themselves in full sympathy with white landlords.

Yes, you only know the feel of a sting when you experience it for yourself. That's to say that only when a black person becomes a landlord and goes through the experience of accommodating his own fellow blacks, can he fully appreciate the white man's dilemma in housing them. Until then, he'll always be one of those blacks ignorantly accusing white landlords of colour prejudice. And indeed, when we bear in mind the great grudge my fellow men have against white people, and their deliberate misinterpretation of every petty and innocent matter as being directed against their colour, we have to acknowledge that white landlords who are prepared to house them must surely be in an even greater dilemma than ever. How do they approach the sensitive black tenants without the latter reacting emotionally and accusing them of being colour prejudiced? . . . I've listened to black people tell of rows they had with white landlords, who apparently repeatedly approached them for being noisy and untidy when that wasn't the case at all. The complainants claimed the landlords were plain racialists, and, they added, told them so directly. Partly out of tact, partly because I knew I'd be in a hair-raising row myself if I tried to question or doubt their story, I never did so.

I only remember one occasion when a white landlady and I discussed black tenants. This was in a small, cheap West London hotel where I lodged for two months preceding my moving into Lewisham. On my second morning there, I went downstairs to the elegant TV lounge to find the young bespectacled housekeeper, an affable and naïve-looking Irish wife, occupied with her cleaning. First a little chit-chat, then rather hesitantly she enquired if I was afraid that I would encounter colour prejudice in the hotel. Puzzled by the question I said: 'no'. She closed her eyes with a smile of relief, saying softly: 'Thank God.' Whereupon she started a long explanation. Her three months as housekeeper there had seen six black tenants, and all but one had been nightmares till the day they left. Apparently, they had come with the rigid conception that they would be victimised for being black. Day in and day out they raised hell, constantly criticising the hotel's services and the conditions of lodging, rudely approaching the management about lost property and insinuating theft: yet on recovering lost items, never apologising for their wrongful suspicions. They remained convinced that everybody—the white lodgers and the management—was colour prejudiced, and often threatened to report to the Race Race Relations Board. They picked rows with everybody, and two of them on separate occasions were in a punch-up with white tenants.

The voice of my narrator was jerky as she spoke—evidence that she was feeling awkward saying all this. I believed every word she said, accepting her assurance that neither she nor her husband had any racial bias whatever. My fellow men had a chip and were far too sensitive, she stated, and stressed: 'They just seem to come *looking* for trouble.' I agreed and expressed my sympathy to her. Needless to say, I personally never encountered any colour prejudice during my stay at the hotel.

Yes, black people in England do enjoy looking for trouble. I clearly remember that in six different restaurants (one Chinese, three Indian and two take-away shops) life had been peaceful until black people came in and started a scene. For example, a well-dressed African of about forty came into an Indan restaurant one afternoon to order take-away food and sat down at a table meant for diners. When the young Indian waiter politely asked if he could wait at the table specially reserved for take-away orders, he started to shout and protest that he should be allowed to sit wherever pleased him. He called it cheek that the Indian should tell him where to sit, and demanded to see the manager—who was not there. The Indian's attempt to reason with this African was useless, and the latter angrily cancelled his order and stormed out. There were only a few other diners, who all kept silent. When the Indian served me, he quietly expressed his incomprehension at the African's behaviour. With amiable triviality I replied that the best way to treat an ignorant man was to ignore him.

On another occasion it was in a large fish-and-chip shop late one Saturday night. There was a long queue, and service was going swimmingly until a small group of scruffy West Indian youths entered. They went straight to the counter. When the counter-hand reminded them that there was a queue, one shouted viciously: 'Piss off, man! We know there is a fucking queue. We don't have to join it.' Whereupon the rest of the gang assailed the counter-hand with insults. The counter-hand kept his mouth shut. There was no reaction from any of the customers.

On the other occasions when blacks started trouble in restaurants it was usually over the meals they ordered: a little mistake on the part of the waiter. But what was so off-putting was that the blacks saw fit to draw everybody's attention by being blatantly rude to the waiters, when the matter could so easily have been settled quietly. In all the public eating places I've been, no member of a non-black race caused a scene— just blacks. This is what disturbs me most about the whole thing. Why must it be only blacks? It just makes no sense at all. As another example, not long ago I went to the New Victoria cinema in South London to watch a Cassius Clay boxing match which was being shown live on close-circuit television. It was about 2 am. The place was packed. Just before the show started, as guests poured in to take their seats, pandemonium struck!

There was a great scene going on at the entrance door. It sounded like a big fight. A voice was shouting: 'No, you're not going in. You'll get me sacked!' What was it all about? A group of people were trying to force their way in without tickets. And who else could it be but black people! They never got in. The police were called and they were taken away. I remember also that at the end of the show there was yet more trouble outside. A crowd listened to this elderly, light-skinned Asian miserably complain to the police that his ticket had been forcibly taken off him and he never saw the fight. The accused was a young West Indian in his mid-twenties—who simply denied the accusation. The two men were driven off to the police station to dispute the issue there.

Somehow, I haven't given up hope that the day will come when my fellow men will examine themselves and realise that they encounter prejudice here much more because of their troublesome nature than because of their colour. All I can do is hope. The inclination to try criticising or reasoning with them has long since abandoned me. Because the self-pitying souls consider themselves as being totally blameless regarding the racial palaver in the world, to try and get them to accept any form of criticism on race is as futile as a bishop attempting to lecture the Mafia.

I remember the day at Speakers' Corner when I was listening to a group of blacks rave on about their sufferings in England. Though I normally attended these speeches in silence, I backed up the courage to confront the chief spokesman.

'Don't you think black people sometimes do look for trouble?' I asked. But is my question answered? Never. Volcanic mouths spouted lavas of insults and I was shoved from all sides by angry hands. My heart somersaulting with a passion of excitement, I was determined to make my point. With exaggerated calmness, I loudly expressed my thought that this country was too tolerant towards black people, then suggested that they might examine themselves and see if they weren't in some way to answer for their hardships. I was barracked and drenched with all the obscenities under the sun. I lost courage. Overwhelmed by irritation and apprehension, I left without another word. It was like trying to reason with a pack of wild animals. I have remained surprised that I emerged out of all that unscathed.

On another occasion, a similar incident was too farcical for words. A group of loud-mouthed blacks were happy to agree with a hypothetical suggestion that their fellow men in South Africa would soon eject the whites from the country. A quiet, smartly-dressed black, carrrying the atmosphere of importance, questioned this.

'How do you make that out?' he said with dignified casualness. 'So far as I can see the blacks in South Africa do not at the moment have the means to throw out the whites.'

For saying this, he was reviled most vociferously by the others and dismissed as being brainless and beneath notice. The poor man, really shaken by this verbal bombardment being piled on his head, stood there dumbfounded—till a bearded half-caste, a doctor whom I knew well, came to his defence. With a convincing display of logic, he protested: 'Look, none of you have answered this man his question! . . . That is, how do you foresee the blacks ousting the whites from South Africa?'

With snarling fierceness, one black stormed: 'Man, what the hell are you talking about? Of course they will, man. Look at Angola. Weren't the blacks once held down by the Portuguese there? . . . We've risen up now, and we're belting the hell out of them. Haven't you heard that Portugal has had to keep sending more troops to help their men? We'll soon deal with the whites in South Africa as well, man!' Many voices agreed.

'Wait,' answered the doctor, still unsatisfied, 'what is your source of information about Portugal? I've heard no news of any troop movement from Portugal to Angola within the last six months....'

Whereupon the other lost his temper and burst out screaming: 'Informer! Secret agent! You come to find out how I obtain my information then go and tell Foreign Office.' He started to walk away, attracting much attention by looking back, pointing and shouting: 'Informer! Be careful of that man, he is a secret agent!'

My fellow men look all the more stupid when, on finding themselves cornered with valid criticisms or convincing points, they try and break out with that barbaric method of the caveman—violence. At Speakers' Corner one afternoon, I was in a hot dispute with two West Indians. They insisted that much as the Caribbean was now their home, they were still Africans. I conceded that there were few differences between the two races: mannerisms, mentality, general outlook and tastes were all basically the same. But owing to the great passage of time since the West Indians were shipped away from Africa, they had lost complete contact with the African culture and way of life, and could never fit in or be accepted in Africa. So in no way could they be called Africans. The argument raged on. My opponents shouted furiously in a vain effort to win my agreement—till one became tired and went away. As the other and I thrashed out the issue, one of the few auditors— a wizened old Englishman in a dark suit and hat—joined in and sided with me. And blow me down!—with the cool, specious confidence of a professional, this old Charlie, within a minute, was able to crush every ounce of verbal resistance from my opponent's lips. And the latter—a burly, middle-aged six-footer of very smart appearance—in a controlled temper called

Charlie Boy an ignoramus, placed one enormous hand on his face and powerfully shoved him. I held the assailant back, gently asking him to cool it. Charlie Boy, naturally shaken, stood there with unconcealed apprehension. His assailant abused him once more, and we went our separate ways. When I reflected on the matter a while later, I saw the assault as being pointless and unjustified. It proved nothing. Similarly another occasion when an elderly, bespectacled English lady was assaulted by a black man. She had angrily tried to defend the whites against the accusations made by the Asian orator. And as blacks shouted at the orator to ignore her, one turned in a fit of temper, wrenched the spectacles from her face and flung them aside. As fellow blacks cooled him down, the old lady snapped protests at him, then retrieved her spectacles and went. And that was that.

Thus the black man's typical reactions when involved in arguments. Whenever I remember that aphorism by the writer Voltaire, I feel pleasure and admiration: 'I hate what you say, but will defend to the death your right to say it.' But with the black man, it seems, should he hate what you say, he will probably fight you to death for daring to say it. I'll never cease to wonder why, if my fellow men really see themselves as the sympathetic and innocent victims of the racial tension today, they shouldn't be only too happy to listen to criticisms and opposing views. Perhaps they could then—by using the faculty of reasoning—convince their opponents of the validity of their claims. Violence, aggression and insults surely won't deflect anybody's opinions. These, really, are shields to hide one's defeat and one's pain and refusal to accept defeat. Indeed such reactions suggest stupidity: suggest that they haven't the intelligence to try and resolve an issue sensibly. White people, quite justifiably, get an image of us as being brainless brutes. This my fellow men resent—yet at the same time are ready to display their brainlessness with their violent habits.

So now consider. You're keen to settle your differences with somebody who sees himself as being completely innocent, holding you responsible for everything. When you try and challenge him about this he reacts emotionally and won't listen to you. Where's your hope of ever reaching some sort of rational understanding with him? This is the situation between the whites and blacks in this country today, and it is merely one of the reasons why the two races will never live together in peace and quiet. Only my fellow men can cure the situation— simply by bearing in mind that as they are the ones crying out to be accepted in a white country, it's necessary that they abandon their resorts to violence and start learning to reason. Certainly violence is necessary at times to deal with words. Insulting language, for instance, can quite justifiably be dealt with by violence. When a person tries to hurt you with words, you're within your rights to hurt him in any way you wish. But to resolve a simple argument, violence is a complete failure, and will only succeed in heightening the tension between the opponents.

My fellow men's quick temper explains why I've stopped trying to argue with them about race. It's my views on race which have made my efforts to reintegrate with them disastrous. I had no qualms about making my feelings about black people known. The black man was an animal! Dirty! Stupid! Inferior to the white man! Whenever present in a company of black acquaintances during a discussion on race, I made these statements. You should have seen their fury. Time has taken me through a frightful journey of rows, on four occasions introducing punch-ups, and near punch-ups on numerous instances.

Intermediaries always stepped in and halted the fights. Except for one occasion when my watch and glasses were badly smashed, I always emerged unscathed. The number of my opponents who ever bothered to ask *why* I believed the statements I made before losing their tempers was one out of ten! Frequently the inevitable nickname has been screamed in my ears—John Bull's Nigger!—which, incidentally, means an English-loving black person, the famous American equivalent being 'Uncle Tom's'. You can never win with the black man. You allow yourself to view a situation from the white man's angle as well, and you are at once accused of wishing to be white yourself. Don't for one moment think that the blacks who take this selfish attitude are the ignorant or ill-educated bunch. Not at all. Most of my opponents have been very much the opposite, and well above average intelligence. Many have been students and graduates of English universities. Certainly, I love the white man—but only because he lives and acts like the human being nature created him to be. Often I've made this crystal clear to my opponents. God knows that I don't love the white man for the colour of his skin. God knows, too, that I would have no preference to be white. I've failed to get most of my opponents to believe this. No doubt I worsened the situation by a stupid action I once embarked upon. I strolled along to a black barber's shop in Marble Arch one afternoon and had my hair straightened—just like a white man's. I just did it for kicks, and was also curious to feel the difference between curly hair and straight hair. The reactions from black people were, of course, harsh. At Speakers' Corner, at my Bayswater hostel, and even in the streets, I underwent endless taunts, abuse and accusations of wishing to be white. 'Why don't you also get a bleaching powder and bleach yourself white!' This sort of taunt was flung in my face again and again by irate blacks.

73

Many—relations and good friends of mine included—dissociated themselves from my company. But I wasn't worried. I regarded the reason for everybody's wrath as being irrational and childish. Just because 'those loathsome white people' had straight hair, and here I was, it seemed, trying my best to look like them. I couldn't understand why I should want to copy the *white* people in particular. Indians had straight hair. So did the Chinese. In fact, the world had more non-whites with straight hair than whites. Why then this obsession about white people's hair? I used to hurl out these points in my defence. But all the blacks remained convinced that I was 'trying to be white'. None, however, could offer me just *one* reason why I should imitate the whites of all people. Obviously, my fellow men hated my action because to them it suggested that I wasn't proud of my origin. I was virtually acknowledging that being black was a misfortune. And this was as good as abusing them.

However, I got used to their criticisms and insults. My typical, cool-headed reply when often asked to explain myself: 'Time is changing, so why not change with time?' And on occasions when irritation did overwhelm me, I shouted: 'I know that the blacks wish to remain backwards. But I want to change.' Not really meant, of course. The one criticism which made me regret my action was: 'That wasn't how God made you.' I wasn't honest enough to admit it, so I was never without some sort of a reply: 'What the hell do you know about how God made me? . . . Didn't God endow man with the power to improve himself as he sees fit? . . . Did God design us blacks to be so idiotic in our outlook? . . .' And, of course, that last statement got me into rows.

The one person I couldn't really argue with was my old man. Relatives wrote to inform him of my action. He, in turn, stopped my visits to Holland till my hair was in its natural condition. It

74

took three months before my hair, with regular trimming by me, grew into its natural, tight curls. It wasn't so much my old man's wrath that made me change. It was more that shame and regret, with no logical explanation, convinced me that it was wrong not to remain my natural self. Besides, I wasn't impressed with my straight hair. It was always dish-evelled. Curly hair remained unruffled in any situation—in bed, in the rain and in the wind.

To end the topic, I might add that I was also criticised by white people for my action. Some of them succeeded in antagonising me. They, too, thought that by straightening my hair I was craving to look like them. Such conceit really beat hell out of me. I made them understand that there were other races who had straight hair. When I angrily asked why I should be trying to 'look white', none of them, either, could offer any reason. The obvious explanation is that in this very race-conscious world, where almost every act is given racial under-tones, such a gesture as mine would automatically join the bandwagon. Inevitably, it would be associated with 'the white man', since the whites have always held the upper hand in the long-standing racial tension between them and my fellow men. However, the fact that both blacks and whites accused me of wanting to be 'white' is a golden example of the 'inferiority' and 'superiority' complexes that are paramount in the two races.

As I said, I don't want to be white. I like to remain black, and I wish I could be proud of it. But right now I can't be—not with my fellow men's present behaviour. The only way they can improve is to be badgered with criticism and made to see the truth about themselves. This is more hopeful than letting them remain lost in their false thoughts that they are entirely inno-cent in the racial palaver in the world. And the only person who could bring them to accept criticisms and seriously question their validity is none but a sincere black 'brother' who is anxious for their advancement yet knows that they are to blame for their retrogression through their own stupidity.

4

WE'VE HEARD A LOT ABOUT WHITE PEOPLE'S injustices to blacks in this country. My fellow men always make sure that their sufferings are publicised. But we seem to be spared news about the grievances whites suffer from blacks. Though it seems that only blacks are victimised, we should look to see if there are whites who do suffer at the hands of black people. For a long time I've watched the indignities particular white folks have suffered from my fellow men: indignities that are never brought to public notice. The victims are white girls.

To begin, I'll relate the ordeal of a French girl in London. She was raped by a black man. I knew the rapist personally—an arrogant, powerfully-built Nigerian studying at a university in England. His victim, a shapely brunette in her late twenties, was, in fact, a recent girl-friend of a young, handsome black salesman also from Nigeria. I'll just call him Bob. He was a friend of mine; a quiet, but very witty fellow. His acquaintance with his girl-friend's rapist had been brief, but he had come to like and trust him. The rapist had made the girl believe Bob was waiting for her at the bed-sitter where he was spending his holidays. His deceit was soon exposed after they arrived home in his car. Inside his room he made his advances. She fought at first until, terrified by his vicious threats of violence, submitted while he stripped and raped her. Later, she stumbled through her boyfriend's door and collapsed sobbing in his arms. Slenderly-built Bob, enraged and disillusioned, lost no time in calling the police. The rapist, however, couldn't be found. Bob's enquiries through black friends were fruitless. Eventually, he found himself persuading his girl-friend to drop the charges. He was influenced by one of his fellow men's suggestions. They felt sympathy for him and condemned the rapist's action. But hell! It was only a *white* girl! Why make such a fuss and try to ruin a fellow black's career for the sake of a white girl?—particularly as you are both good friends. Had it been a black girl, cause for complaint. But hell! A white girl? Forget it, man. Wasn't this the game the slave-masters repeatedly played on our black 'sisters'? And what was done about it? ... She's not worth the bother, man. She's not your wife; you aren't even in love with her. So what the hell is she to you? ... That the rapist victimised a fellow *black's* girl-friend makes it particularly mean and betrayal of him, cruel. Had it been a white guy's, okay; but not a fellow black's. Get hold of the rapist and beat him black and blue—or get others to do it for you. But don't use the white pigs to ruin a black 'brother's' life for the mere sake of a white girl. It's not good, man.

That was the attitude of Bob's black friends. He was, however, only prepared to consider the point that the rapist was a great academic with bright hopes for the future. It would be rather a shame to ruin his chances in life. But for that reason, Bob would have had no mercy. The matter happened some two years ago. I was on holiday in Holland at the time, and was brought into the picture by Bob on my return. I admired his leniency, as I imagine that had I been in his shoes, I would never have slept properly till the rapist was behind bars—however friendly we were, whatever his hopes for the future. The rapist was a very sociable fellow who always holidayed in London. Since that incident I've never seen or heard of him.

Bob considered his fellow men's reason that he should overlook his girl-friend's ordeal because she was white as being
irrational and childish. He gave it no consideration at all. She
was a delightful girl, he was fond of her, and so he cared.

That rape and the reaction of Bob's friends are characteristic
of many black people in England. White girls also suffer their
resentment. I shudder to try and remember the number of
times I've heard this sort of remark from black people: 'White
girls are no good. Don't waste a penny on them. Just give them
a good screw and drop them. That's all they're good for.' And
should the girls refuse to 'play bingo', my fellow men would
most likely turn to aggression and rape. This has been the
experience of a number of white girls I've personally known.
Take Sheila for one. She was a tall American blonde in her
early twenties, whose drowsy face wore a sort of sad maturity:
a girl who tended to trust people too much. I can't recall
how long she'd lived in London when we met but I think it
was a matter of months. Apart from myself, one other black
had had the opportunity of dating her. That brief friendship was given a dramatic ending. After dining out together
one evening, both returned to her host's flat for drinks. Time
passed unnoticed, and it became very late. Sheila accepted her
host's invitation to stay the night: he needn't drive her all the
way home. Presently, the façade he had so far maintained
began to slide away. Temptation seized him. First a vain
effort to get her drunk, followed closely by seduction. Sheila
wasn't prepared to be rushed into intercourse after only one
evening's acquaintanceship, but her host was past caring. He
flung himself on her, and the next few minutes saw them both
in a violent struggle on the floor, the host determined to rape
her, Sheila damned if he would. A girl of great self-control, she
tried to reason with him rather than scream. She emerged the

winner. And the host, furious at her determination and his own failure, became very abusive and ordered her out of his flat. It was a bitingly cold night. This and the bad reputation of that area (the notorious Portobello Road in West London's Notting Hill Gate), froze her desire to step outside alone. Expressing her fear to her host, she begged that he drive her home. He refused—unless he could enjoy her body. Sheila remained unyielding, somehow captured the courage and went. It was fear and tension all the way up the lengthy road, but she safely reached the main road and got a taxi. Remarkably enough, she had no bitter feelings about the matter: just relieved that her host was unsuccessful in his attempted rape.

Of the other white girls I knew who couldn't be seduced in haste by anybody, who had found blacks the most persistent, unreasonable and violent men, two more were raped by blacks: one, a timid Austrian *au pair* because she was too afraid to resist; the other, an English London University student whose drunkenness deprived her of sufficient strength to fight off her triumphant rapist. Neither took any action against their rapists. Not one of the other more fortunate white girls could forget the insults they took from blacks for their refusal to have sex. Another girl I know paid dearly for her refusal. She was an attractive blonde whom I'll call Gloria. Black people repel her! This was because of the shameful torture she suffered from a black man who took her out for the first time. From the pub they went to his flat. There Gloria soon found herself rebuffing his sexual advances. This proved a fatal mistake. He virtually turned paranoiac. Mouthing obscenities, he stormed out into the kitchen and shortly emerged with an unhygienic, splintered plunger. Like some possessed demon, he overpowered and stripped the terror-stricken Gloria, and with this plunger violated her. So appalling were her injuries that the doctors thought it a miracle that she didn't bleed to death. Her injuries became infected. She was in hospital for seven weeks and underwent a major operation—the total removal of her womb. As a result she can never have any children. Of course, the police were called. But despite their persistent questioning and pleading, Gloria refused to name her assailant. Apparently he belonged to a gang of ruthless thugs, and she'd been warned to keep quiet, otherwise a very intimate friend of hers—a girl I know well—would be murdered. Gloria knew that this threat was no idle one. So her assailant remains a free man today; but thanks to his 'considerate service', black people have won his victim's hatred.

Yes, *only* white girls will black men treat like this. Before we examine the reasons more deeply, I can't resist relating one verbal exchange which serves as another perfect example of my fellow men's disrespect of white girls. It took place one cold November night in 1971, a night enveloped by thick fog. I was in the neat little sitting-room of a West Indian's semi-detached house. He was a fat, married man around thirty years of age; a lazy, loud-mouthed adulterer who dishonestly lived off social security when quite well off financially—and boasted about it. As we both lounged on his sofa, glued to a tedious television programme, he sighed with irritation and boredom, then crudely suggested that he and I go out hunting for white girls to rape. When I told him to stop being absurd, I realised with astonishment that he meant it. The thick fog, he reckoned, was to our advantage, coupled with the basic myth in the white men's thinking that all blacks look alike. The girls would have no hope of identifying us. We could drag them somewhere convenient and give them a good raping, he added. The white bitches, that was all they deserved. Announcing that he was crazy, I turned down his idea. And that was that.

Similarly, I've often met blacks who encourage one another to use aggression to make unwilling white girls submit to sex. And should their attempts be futile, whatever else be as rude as possible. I know a number of black men who do this all the time. Some not only become aggressive and abusive, but try and get refunded the cost of the girls' entertainment.

So we ask ourselves: what is it about white girls which blinds so many black men with this abnormal desire to conquer them sexually to the extent that they would attempt rape? The truth is that white girls, in their eyes, are far more attractive than their own black girls. I imagine my fellow men have the same sort of feelings for white girls as I have. To me the white girl is like a goddess of beauty. It's not just the fact that she's a woman that I love. I love her smooth, tender white skin. Look at that soft, silky hair; that gracefully, flowing hair. What could be a more beautiful sight than a white woman's hair being blown in the wind? ... There's a delicate softness about her that I simply can't explain: a softness that makes her seem so holy: a softness that would send me hurtling over a hundred black girls just to reach her. When she lies submissively on my bed exposing her naked body, she makes my flesh cry out for hers, makes my desire a burning torture, and my need for her irresistible. There's no such thing as an ugly white girl; even if she's bald-headed, cross-eyed and only has one black tooth, she's still beautiful.

Put a black girl on my bed, however, and all my personal instincts would rebel. Here's the goddess of ugliness. The black girl is a loud-mouth, a hard-muscled machine full of vigour and resistance—too much on the masculine side: not quiet, weak, gentle and submissive like the white girl. If I piled the black girl, my eyes would tightly shut as I fought to imagine it was a luscious white blonde struggling vigorously against me. That's the only possible way I could reach climax with a black girl. Should I happen to see the boisterous black face or my hand feel the rough, frizzy curls, my attempts to enjoy myself would come to an abrupt end. I would be better off stopping, for even if I spent the whole day invading her, I'd never get any satisfaction. I imagine this is how I'd feel, as I've not made any sexual conquest of a black girl since I was ten. And having come to adore the beauty of the white girl so passionately after all these years, I've lost all physical desire for black girls—for now; but that will not, I fancy, always be so. In moons to come when I'm older and wiser, I'll probably look back to my present attitude towards the black girl and dismiss it as being childish. You never know.

This attitude towards the black girl is personal, and I certainly don't speak for other black men—most of whom do find their own girls physically attractive. But it would be the height of dishonesty if they tried to deny that they recognise the white girl as being more attractive than the black girl: if they tried to deny that they feel the same way as I do about the white girl— the only difference being that most of them respect her physical beauty alone: for them, a thing to be enjoyed. And when they find they can't enjoy that 'thing', they become resentful. For 'something' as precious as the *white* girl to be denied them cuts their feelings like a knife. Instinctively, thoughts of the slave-days are awakened, of white racialists, of white girls being defiled by blacks and shunning them. The white bitch! Accursed yet so beautiful. Her rebuff strengthens the black man's sexual desire for her all the more. As they say: 'The unobtainable is the most desirable.' Oh, how can she be had? The black man's resentment is diminished by ideas of rape—the only way to achieve his desire. Otherwise, he accepts her refusal, but becomes rude. This wipes the painful feeling of being rebuffed from his system and gives him the grim satisfaction of hurting her feelings as she has done to his, at the same time making her seem small and inferior for a change.

It's clear that most blacks suspect racial undertones when white girls say no to sex. Most of such girls I've known believed this, with assurances that the question of colour differences never entered their heads. With some it was simply not in their nature to make love with men till they knew each other better, whilst with the others particular blacks didn't appeal to them physically—just as any white man may not attract a girl physically. Our sympathy must reach out for the white girls who find themselves in this awkward situation with black men. And the blacks who see fit to practise such unjust treatment should know better, as it won't help to win the respect from white people that they always seek.

You'll never cease to shudder when you hear how many black men treat white girls who do become involved with them. It's atrocious! Having acquired the girls' infatuation, having thoroughly known their flesh, the black men now have this sadistic desire to see them look ugly and wretched: to see those proud faces fall into petulant frowns of pain and fright. They assume the role of the white slave-masters, and treat white girls like the black women were treated in the slave-days. They subject them to the most base humiliations, mete out brutalities and generally impose fear upon them. Should the girls become pregnant, too bad!—the blacks don't want to know. I've got used to hearing black people boast about their own such exploits, emphasising that white girls only deserved such treatment. I've befriended many white girls who suffered such hardships, and I've seen some nasty scenes.

Here's an experience I had in Lewisham. I was walking down the road from the railway station one cold, dusky evening.

84

Reaching the junction of the busy street, I came across this tramp-like woman with her half-caste kid, loitering around with no apparent aim. Both were in a filthy state—evidence that theirs was a world of squalor. The woman was youngish, her grime-covered face registering the agony of lengthy suffering. My attention happened to be directed at them for some moments when, all of a sudden, the woman screamed out: 'Yeah, 'ave a bloody good look, you fucking wog!' Her voice was bitter and somewhat hysterical. This unexpected outburst startled me into stopping. I eyed her enquiringly for a few seconds, then shook my head with dumb incomprehension and quietly walked on. This seemed to antagonise her even more, and further abuse followed me round the corner: 'Bloody nigger! Go home!' I could feel staring eyes, of course, but I had enough confidence in myself not to feel embarrassed. Also, insults no longer bothered me, so I wasn't hurt by her words. There and then I couldn't understand why she seemed so bitter. But, later, on remembering her half-caste kid, their miserable state, everything became clear. The poor woman had been in love with some cruel, black guy whose manner of returning that love was to enslave and brutalise her, give her a child and leave her to struggle pennilessly on her own. This was the effect it had on the woman—bitterness and hatred for black people.

As I thought about the matter that night, I reminded myself that my fellow men will still complain that they are hated only because they are black, and don't deserve the Englishman's hatred. I got rocks in my stomach just thinking about *the black man*. When, I wondered, would he escape from Satan's influence? My mind felt too exhausted to probe that question further as it triggered off memories of other white girls who had experienced my fellow men's brutalities. There was one very gregarious girl named Janeen, a neat, smooth-faced cockney blonde. Tall and fleshy, she was an eighteen-year-old office clerk who wasn't altogether a happy girl. A series of disappointing relationships with three black youths were responsible. Never, incidentally, had she been dated by white boys. Her first two black boy-friends apparently enjoyed beating her. During a visit to my Lewisham home one evening, she lifted her skirt to show me the appalling bruises caused by her second boy-friend during a recent fight. Much as she found black people too violent, it wasn't so much her boy friends' violent nature that she resented; for, having had a tough, working-class upbringing, she was used to rough treatment and always fought back. Her chief complaint was that her boy-friends were unbearably domineering, always wanting things their own way. She was convinced they only liked her body, while as a person, she was beneath notice or respect. She was taken out only as a show-piece, she felt, and their whole disrespectful attitude depressed her. Her third boy-friend, however, raised sparks of hope in her heart. Non-violent, non-domineering. But alas! She was convinced that he, too, felt nothing for her as a person: merely saw her as a body and a show-piece. When I took Janeen to a pub in New Cross some time ago, she was sad to confess that their four-month relationship was badly deteriorating, and that the final break-up was imminent. What I considered the juicy meat of our conversation was her grave statement that her future relationships would only be with white boys. She had carefully considered the matter and decided she would be happier being dated by fellow whites. I really felt sympathy for her.

One question I've never resisted asking white girls I've come to know is if they have ever been dated by black men. With many of these girls the answer was no. Whereupon I discouraged them from ever attempting the experience. I never bluntly stated that they should shun black men, but I fancy

86

they got the message; I merely suggested that they should be very cautious of them. I used to describe the indignities white girls suffered from my fellow men, explaining that the former's physical aspects were the only attraction for most blacks. All my girl-friends were naturally appalled. I think they heeded my warning; and should they ever be approached by black men, they'll watch it. You may think me a devil for what I did, but many of those girls were very nice characters, and I couldn't bear to imagine my fellow men returning their friendly gestures with ill-treatment that would surely turn them into 'nigger haters'.

So there it is. Many white girls show that they have no racial bias whatever by readily befriending black men, who, in exchange, turn them into racialists with their unjustified ill-treatment. If they only realised the image they give the black race, they'd perhaps refrain from such pointless and grotesque practices.

I could relate many more cases where white girls have refused to go out with blacks again following nasty experiences. This one happened in Liverpool. For the first time in her life, a pretty, nineteen-year-old brunette started a relationship with a black man. He was a tall African of twenty-one whom she found very well-mannered: not surprising, since he had had the benefit of a public school education. (And it wasn't me, incidentally.) All went well for the first three weeks, then it happened! They both left the Saturday-night disco around 2 am. It was a fine, moonlit summer's night. He took her to a nearby alleyway, and there subjected the unsuspecting girl to the most heinous humiliation. He started to strip her. She let him, thinking he wanted to make love. But no. Leaving her wearing only pants, he took her clothes to a puddle of water nearby, dropped them in and proceeded to stamp on them till they were thoroughly saturated with mud and water. He then laughed in her face and left. The poor girl, almost paralysed with shocked disbelief, stood huddled in humiliation, shaking from head to foot. Next moment she was sobbing with rage and self-pity. Luckily, she was overheard by an old couple in a small house nearby. An anxious granny came out to investigate, saw the pitiful sight and was very sympathetic. She gently led the victim into the house, where she and her husband made her feel at home, dried her clothes and put her up till dawn. The girl simply told them that she had been assaulted, but insisted, when her hosts suggested it, that she didn't want the police called. Her hosts could never guess, of course, that the reason was that her assailant was a steady boy-friend whom she had been very fond of. The boy-friend, a self-supporting individual of wealthy parents, was the only black in his circle of friends and was popular. His act circulated like bush-fire, and *all* his friends, his girl-friend included, of course, disconnected themselves from him. He was ostracised, but well armed with arrogance and self-confidence, he was beyond caring.

Why did he subject his girl-friend to such treatment? 'Just for the sheer thrill of it,' Shirley, the narrator, told me. 'He doesn't like white girls: he brags that he can get any white girl he wants and make a fool of her.' Shirley was a strikingly beautiful girl in her mid-twenties with dark, flowing hair; a gregarious, freckled Anglo-Spaniard, trim as a bird, who had travelled the world five times. She knew the African assailant and his girl-friend well, and lived in that part of Liverpool when the incident happened. She had once liked the assailant, but: 'I really hated him for what he did to that girl, the arrogant swine,' she told me contemptuously when I once visited her homely South London flat. The boy's girl-friend, as a result of her experience, swore never to go near a black man again. 'And can you blame her, poor girl?' Shirley said. I had to agree. 'He had been so liked and respected by all of us,' she went on. 'Nobody ever noticed his colour until that incident, then their attitude towards him changed....' Several months after that incident, Shirley had met him at a dance party. He approached, held her in a hug, and started to flatter her about her beauty. Then with polite sauciness, he said: 'My God, Shirley, if ever I got you in an alleyway, I'd make love to you and do exactly what I did to that girl.' And Shirley, an intelligent but rather insecure girl, told him obscenely to get lost—which he did.

Shirley herself didn't trust black men. She was friendly with a good number, but was never involved with one. That African's act was just one of many grievances black men inflicted upon white girls she knew. So she was very cautious of them. She wanted men to respect her as a person as well as a body, but the blacks she knew all seemed to be after just the one thing ... 'And also,' she explained in a rather innocent way, 'I've discovered that many of your people are fond of making white girls pregnant and running off.' Gracious me, I could probably tell her more about that, was my reply.

So much for what I've heard about my fellow men's ill-treatment of white girls, what have I actually seen? Not much, I regret to say—no, wait! What am I talking about?—I'm *happy* to say: I don't enjoy seeing such things. However on a number of occasions, I've suffered the shame of witnessing black men create a scene in the streets by screaming insults at their white girl-friends. I imagine they must have felt proud to show the world that *they* were the bosses of *white* girls. Similarly, the two occasions on which I witnessed black men slap their white girl-friends in public for arguing with them: once at a black night club in London's West End, when the teenage girl rushed off sobbing to the 'Ladies': once at Speakers' Corner, when the young lady, surely in her late twenties, was too proud to cry but instantly acceded to her boy-friend's order to return to his home and wait. On both occasions there were no reactions from the onlookers. I've often been told of similar public humiliations by black men of white girls. When I think that the former completely overlook the fact that such behaviour will bring disrepute on them, I find it quite sickening!

Of course, I'm not claiming that all black men in England brutalise white girls, but MANY do. You'll probably wonder why you never seem to hear anything of such injustices. Simply because these white girls are tolerant. They endure black men's ill-treatment and say nothing, much as they are naturally hurt and bitter. What a contrast to black people themselves—who certainly wouldn't let the slightest maltreatment by white folks escape public notice. They may well suffer injustices from white people, but it should be made known that some white folks do suffer terribly at their hands. When you consider that the prejudice they encounter in this country is mild, and they will, nevertheless, always create a furore, you must wonder what they would create if this prejudice took the same form as that which they themselves inflict upon white girls. This country would become a blood bath.

What I find most laughable of all is the hypocrisy in my fellow men's continual preference to date white girls, which now seems commonplace in England. As my fellow men's famous dictum—'Black is beautiful. I'm black and proud'—informs us, they have been mentally overwhelmed by the obsession to eradicate that image carved in their minds by the white slave-masters that the white girl is the sole symbol of beauty. The tree of determination has taken root in their minds to recognise black girls as possessing a superior beauty to their white counterparts. But the fact that the tree of their desire still offers more seeds to white girls than to black ones is a confession that failure is triumphant in their so-called epitaph 'Black is beautiful'. In their subconscious the white girl still wears the crown. What blind hypocrisy! Consequently, the apparent envy and dislike of black girls against their white counterparts grow more bitter as time goes on. They resent their own men's hypocrisy, but unfortunately there's little they can do about it except (to add the old proverb): 'If you can't beat them join them.' Subsequently many of them spend indiscriminately in an effort to westernize themselves. They buy cosmetics—consisting of facial creams, powders, hair-straightening materials etc., in an attempt to win the contesting admiration of their men. But few ever achieve full satisfaction. The changes they undertake simply fail to suit their natural appearance. They are black, and are fully aware that whatever happens they'll remain as different from their white counterparts as chalk from cheese. So their envy drags on. Ironically, whereas their men are attracted to white girls, they themselves reserve their admiration solely for their own kind. It's a rare sight to see black girls with white men: partly because they have this clan instinct, partly because the bitter memory is still alive in their subconscious of the bestial submission that their black sisters forcibly underwent to their white slave-masters during their bondage. Black girls surely can't be blamed for being envious of their white counterparts. But there's certainly no reason to excuse black men for showing themselves to be so hypocritical.

5

HYPOCRISY IS A MAJOR FAULT IN THE BLACK
man's character. In virtually all my fellow men's utterances
about race, hypocrisy is visible. Let's start with the blacks in
England. They're always complaining about the white man's
prejudice against them. From all this you would surely believe
that the whites were their worst enemies. Not so at all. Really,
the majority of the blacks are their own worst enemies in
England, and any black man seeking to deny it is a born liar.
Again blind hypocrisy glares out. They're so bitter at the white
man's prejudice that they completely overlook that they themselves are guilty of nearly all the accusations they shower on the
whites. Bitter irony today informs us that they carry out the
very injustices that they protest about on their own people.
White people couldn't really be aware of this fact. You have to
be black *and* living with your own people really to know what
goes on among them. The insinuation, by my fellow men's constant protests at the white man's prejudice, is that they themselves maintain a strict observance of humanity towards one
another. They should be ashamed of such false pretence. Let
me first take this question of basic prejudice. Then let me tell
you that the strength of the tension between the blacks and the
whites compared with that between the Africans and the West
Indians is like comparing the strength of Mickey Mouse to that
of King Kong. This is no exaggeration. Such is the hate between
the Africans and the West Indians that it's difficult to believe.

They're both convinced that each is superior to the other, and accuse one another of disgracing the black race. I've got used to listening to the hatred and low opinions that Africans and West Indians have voiced of each other. Both are very much aware of each other's mutual differences and both keep their distances. The reason for the Africans' 'superiority complex' over the West Indians chiefly exists in the fact that many years ago it was African chiefs who sold them to the white slave-traders. This reason is further inflamed by the fact that most of the West Indians here are poorly educated and only seem capable of performing the most menial and base tasks. The West Indians in turn see the Africans as being primitive and savage, for two main reasons: many illiterate Africans have yet to abandon their livelihood in mud-huts and in the jungle; furthermore, whereas the Africans have a common enemy—the whites in South Africa and Rhodesia—they seem preoccupied with slaughtering one another in their barbaric tribal wars. For these reasons, West Indians regard Africans as being more docile and less intelligent than themselves.

Take it from me, therefore, that it's purely on a superficial basis that both will merrily announce to the world that they are brothers and must unite to fight the white man. Behind the scenes, however, both are burning with the anxiety to remind themselves of their different identities, and have no wish to be connected with one another. Several times at Speakers' Corner, I've witnessed a wrathful exchange of accusations and racial insults between them. I clearly remember three occasions on which black members of audiences stood between small groups of Africans and West Indians ready to settle their disputes with their fists. It used to nauseate me that my fellow men should enact such disgraceful displays for the observance of white people, and I always went away in the heat of the rows.

My feeling regarding the attitude between Africans and West Indians has again been one of nausea. Both clearly show themselves for what they really are—abstract hypocrites! Each would experience such a thrill inside to hear whites voice poor opinions of one another; and each craves to look better than the other in the eyes of the whites—evidence of their feeling of inferiority to the white man. On the times that I talked separately with Africans and West Indians and listened to their hateful criticisms against one another, I never tried to defend either against the other. Indeed, I always supported the two of them—simply because their complaints against each other were true—not to mention that several other shocking crimes were common practices of both. I always voiced the one opinion I hold about the matter: 'As far as I'm concerned *all* blacks are devils'—by that, meaning *both* Africans and West Indians.

Rarely would you find the two living together in private residences. The African and West Indian landlords I've known expressed their aversion to accommodating one another. Both saw each other as being dirty and troublesome, and both have solemnly expressed their preferences to accommodate white tenants. The landlords of my South-East London homes were West Indian. Being an African, I just happened to be lucky to be accepted in that I was well-acquainted with intimates of both landlords, who spoke well on my behalf. Otherwise, the landlords wouldn't have taken me. In due course, as we became more closely acquainted, they told me they were against housing Africans. They deplored the way Africans looked down on West Indians as inferior beings to themselves.

Once again I must repeat that it's difficult for the white man —the outsider—to be aware of the hate between the two. But, believe me, that hate is there, and it is strong!

This is why I consider the Black Power movement in England

to be just one great farce. It will never cease to amaze me how its members could be so unaware of the hypocrisy of their posture. To compare it with Black Power in somewhere like America would be like comparing hell with heaven. We all know what Black Power means in America: that the black man's colour is being used as an excuse to persecute him, and so he has to organise on a basis of colour to fight against that persecution. That he does. But in England the Black Power set-up is absurd. To start with, in a country where the black man has no cause at all, where he has never had it so good, he wants to import an American idea that is suited only to America. But the real farce about the Black Power Movement here is that its members are people of different ethnic origins. You get Chinese, Asians, Blacks—the lot. In fact, I know one *white* youth from Cuba who is a member of the Black Power movement. In a country where the racial dispute is mainly between the blacks and the whites, whereas you'd expect a black man to be the chairman of the Black Power Society, you get, instead, a 'redskin': a character from Guyana of Asian origin. The Movement's concept of black is not colour, but people in the world who are not white. This includes the nations that are supposedly most oppressed by the whites—which are Africa, Asia and Latin America. I can't understand how the members of the Black Power movement can call one another 'brothers' when their countries are more hostile to one another than the whites will ever be to any of them. Since when has China regarded India as a brother? Which Asian would make a fool of himself by trying to claim that the Africans—East Africans especially— see them as brothers? The Africans and West Indians don't want to know each other. It's all pure hypocrisy. In America you'll not see one Chinese or Indian in the Black Power move- ment. Every one of its members is as black as coal. There are

Black Power activists here who are simply people who want recognition, and the only way they can do it is to exploit the racial tension in the world by making unnecessary trouble. They've really got nothing to say. And as the saying goes: 'Children should be seen and not heard.'

Another major example of my fellow men's hypocrisy is to be found in the question of exploitation. Any interest towards helping one another is completely alien to them, and given the slightest chance, they would waste no time in draining every penny from each others' pockets. Landlords are no doubt the worst exploiters in the black communities. For most the only interest is to make as much cash from their tenants as possible, charging exorbitant deposit-fees on furniture for flats and asking for much more rent than the accommodations are worth. Whereas the average white landlord would charge £20 deposit on furniture, his black counterpart would ask for £60! I've viewed rooms offered by black landlords which could best be described as 'holes in the walls', the rent-charges ranging from five to eight pounds a week. What robbery! I was fortunate that the two black landlords I've lived under have been reasonable in their rent. But many black tenants I knew were not so fortunate and were virtually penniless after paying their rents. You'll find that most black tenants would preferably live under white landlords than black ones, not only because the former, comparatively, are reasonable in their rent-charges, but also because they are very patient when tenants fall behind with rent. Black tenants know that very few black landlords are like this. Instantly, they would fall out with such tenants and keep up constant pressure on them for payment. Black tenants also know that black landlords cannot appreciate the meaning of the word LAW. When it becomes clear that their bankrupt tentants can't pay up, and at the same time will not leave their homes, the landlords, disregard the fact that to evict such tenants, they must go to court and obtain an eviction order. The only law known to them is their fists, and their own people always seem to be on the receiving end (few black landlords, incidentally, will accommodate white people). For example, a West Indian landlord had difficulty ousting a black tenant who was a long way behind with his rent. Infuriated, he got another black thug and together they broke into the tenant's flat and gave the poor man such a going over, that they earned themselves a five-year prison sentence apiece. Five years is the sort of sentence for a serious criminal offence, and seldom do cases of assault carry such drastic punishment. So you can imagine the savagery of that beating. The victim was treated in hospital for extensive injuries.

That's one method many black landlords use to throw out bankrupt black tenants—thuggery. Others embark on constant harassment, while others don't hesitate to throw out their tenants' belongings in the streets. And the police are always called in.

Black landlords never do things in a systematic way. Just to feel the bulge of pennies in their pockets, they'll do anything against the law. They know that by law they're supposed to sign tenants' rent books. But very few indeed deal with rent books; and they'll refuse you accommodation if you start insisting that you want a rent book. Because, they know that a rent book serves as evidence of your rent-paying and your security of tenure. Without rent books they can overcharge you, and can avoid paying tax from the rent money. Most black landlords carry on such dishonest practices. One of such landlords I know expressed this flippant opinion: 'To hell with the white man's law! I don't believe in no bloody rent book. If a guy comes for a room asking for rent books, I'll just tell him "I don't give rent books, so no room." Any tenant who starts bull-shitting with me about the law, man, I'll kill him and they can lock me up for as long as they like. No bastard will live in my own house and start telling me what I should do and what I shouldn't do. If he can't trust me enough without my having to sign receipt for his rent, then he can piss off!' That's the typical, money-loving black landlord.

Of course, white people themselves love money and exploit one another. But my fellow men are far more ruthless towards themselves in that game than the whites. Having come to appreciate the value of money, the black man will go to extremes to get it. Should his fellow man be dying next door, he wouldn't offer a penny to aid the man's recovery. My fellow men are so callous towards each other that I find it hard to believe. I've met several West Indian house owners who lent money only on condition that they be repaid one and a half times their loan; and I've met three other blacks—one an African businessman—who only changed cheques if they could take a cut of the money. All of them were so tight-fisted that if their own black friends were bankrupt, any question of their considering leniency became ludicrous.

One disturbing case of exploitation I'll never forget took place during the Nigerian civil war. A London-based citizen of secessionist Biafra wrote a glowing letter home to his loved ones. He had, he claimed, invented a highly effective weapon that would surely bring quick victory to the Biafrans and thus put an end to the ghastly orgy of death taking place there. It would require ten thousand pounds to purchase the essentials needed to make the weapon, he claimed. So could they try their best to raise that sum and send it to him as quickly as possible. His relations naturally took him seriously. This wasn't a child talking, but an intelligent thirty-five-year-old grown up, very close to them and deeply sympathetic towards their plight.

As their beleaguered nation was on the edge of financial exhaustion, they couldn't possibly raise such a sum among themselves. One person who could help, however, was working in Europe—a wealthy and distinguished relation of theirs whom they themselves had been financially dependent upon throughout the war. Overwhelmed by excitement, they wrote to him at once, begging that he offer as much financial assistance as possible. As it happened, he wasn't as gullible as they were and dismissed the matter as poppycock. He knew his 'Inventor' relation only too well not to discern that he was merely out to exploit his people's helpless predicament for base personal gain. I myself knew 'The Inventor' well, a likeable though crafty factory worker who, by night, slogged away at the electrical engineering course he had been unsuccessfully wrestling with for some ten years. However, his dishonest scheme fetched him nothing. It offended me immensely. Here were his own people, dying in their tens of thousands every day from starvation, disease and bullets. Yet he was prepared to try and deprive them of their very last penny. His act was evidence of just how much sympathy he showed towards their dilemma. It is all the more sickening that his action is characteristic of blacks. This is how so many of them would readily treat their own people. And at the same time they'll complain that the white man is only interested in exploiting them.

You can't search for a mote in another person's eye without first removing the bigger mote from your own eye. It's sad that my fellow men aren't intelligent enough to appreciate this. Otherwise they would realise that the whites in England aren't their chief problem, but themselves.

Now and again I've read 'underground' black magazines. Their contents were anybody's guess—bitter, biased and exaggerated reports of white people's prejudicial practices against blacks—mostly cases of harassments and physical assaults by white people, in particular, the police. Before I get down to the basic points I want to make, I'm going to wander a little. Black people aren't always the innocent victims of the alleged police maltreatments we've heard so much about over the years. I've been aware that many of them deliberately make life awkward for the police and look for trouble with them. I've already given two examples of this in my first chapter—their defiant attitude when the police try to do their duty. I've often heard black people discourage one another from ever being polite if the police approached them: always remain hard. At Speakers' Corner I've frequently watched black people obstruct the police and try and stop them arresting or cautioning fellow blacks for starting punch-ups. I know for a fact that similar obstructions go on throughout London. Then there was one Black Power activist, a well-known playwright, who was very leniently given a three-year suspended prison sentence for the serious offence of master-minding a plot to kill British police officers.

These examples show that my fellow men themselves do antagonise the police. I don't doubt that there are many 'bent coppers' who are colour prejudiced and do victimise blacks, but there are also many sympathetic ones who don't. These policemen have duties they have to carry out, and it's unreasonable of black people to become difficult when such officers approach them trying to do their duty as peacefully as possible.

Here's another example of this. An educated black man I know who held a high position in the Race Relations Board was in a quarrel with an English girl at her 'bed-sit' home. When she lost her patience and insisted that he should leave, he refused and slapped her face. The girl was in tears and called the police to remove him, but didn't want to press charges. When the police came, the black fellow became resentful.

With saucy conceit, he announced to the officer: 'Look, you can't victimise me, because I am the ... of the Race Relations Board.' Calmly, the officer reasoned with him: 'Look, we're not victimising you, and it doesn't matter who you are. The fact is that you have just assaulted this young girl and she doesn't want you in her home.' After a few more minutes of defiant arguing, the assailant reluctantly left.

So when I read in black magazines about black people being 'falsely' arrested for obstructing police and resisting arrest, I'm tempted to disbelieve the magazines, as these offences are characteristic of black people. However, though I've had no cause to doubt my fellow men's claims of police harassment and brutality, I personally have never seen any evidence of these maltreatments. For this reason, I'm encouraged to think that they are no more victimised by the police than white folks. Because race is the major issue today, any matters involving race or colour receive far more publicity than non-racial ones. This is why we hear more about the police victimising blacks than whites.

Having touched upon this topic, the point I'm really out to make is that because of black people's hypocrisy, I've seldom felt any sympathy for them on hearing about the maltreatment they suffered from the police. Indeed, even though I don't satisfy my own definition of the word 'sadist', their misfortunes have touched my spirit with pleasure—for the sole reason that I've yet to see them treat their own people any better. Since leaving Eton I've witnessed and heard of far more cases of blacks fighting with one another in public than their fighting with white people. Similarly, the number of serious punch-ups I've seen between blacks is much greater than those between whites, believe it or not. Many of the regular fights that I've seen at Speakers' Corner were between blacks. I've never witnessed any serious injuries as a result of the numerous punch-ups I've seen blacks engage in. But I've heard many accounts of such injuries, with the victims requiring hospital treatment.

I've often heard, too, about blacks being involved in thuggery. But again, they always seem to carry out these practices on themselves rather than on their so-called white enemies. The reasons for most of the acts of thuggery I've heard about were trivial. A typical example was when three black thugs went round to the house of a young black landlord one evening. On answering their call, he was dragged out on to the pavement and beaten till he was a grovelling heap on the ground. He was an experienced freelance journalist, and what had earned him his beating was merely an article he had written in the underground newspaper *IT*, attacking a section of the Black Power movement in London. Apparently, his injuries weren't too serious, he didn't require hospital treatment and took no action about the matter.

Until my fellow men learn to show a bit more humanity towards each other, I've decided not to pay any attention to their complaints against the police.

What I've always considered to be a farce is that black people *totally* overlook the fact that the British police, compared with the police in their motherlands, are models of rectitude. My fellow men fail to notice that they would undergo far worse treatment from their own police. I know this isn't hypocrisy in the proper sense of the word, but for argument's sake I'm treating it as such. Visit any country in Black Africa and the West Indies, and the police not only thrive on being officious, harsh, violent and brutal *for the sheer thrill of it*, but are very prone to bribery. Take as an example, my own country Nigeria, where, as Walter Schwarz tells us in his book *Nigeria*, 'The flagrancy of corruption strikes all Nigerians, who are aware of it almost every day.... In 1964, the Nigerian police, amid favourable publicity, formed an X-Squad to deal with it. But it seemed to make no difference. An ex-policeman, Solomon Jacob, reported in a Lagos newspaper that some X-Squad men arrested some traffic policemen for demanding and receiving money from the members of the public; later these same X-Squad men were arrested by other X-Squad men for demanding and receiving money from the traffic policemen whom they had arrested.'

And for a perfect example of police brutality, we have Haiti, a small Caribbean island with the calamitous population of five million people, nearly all being of pure African descent. As is well known, for the fourteen years since 1957 that the feared voodoo tyrant—the late 'Papa Doc' Françoise Duvalier —was in power, Haiti had been a nightmare world for her inhabitants. Duvalier's famous secret police—the Tonton Macoute—launched an endless campaign of terror that horrified the world. They carried out slaughters, uncurbed thuggery, vile tortures and false arrests of any suspected opponents and critics of Duvalier. And there was absolutely nobody to whom the helpless inhabitants could turn for help.

I dread to imagine what would be the state of affairs among the blacks here if the British police carried out the same prac- tices on them as the police do on the folks in black countries. My fellow men should, at least, be grateful that their protests against the police are always heeded—always the centre of controversy and investigations. Rarely is that the case in black countries.

My fellow men's duty is to learn to analyse themselves. Some self-examination would open their eyes to the fact that not only is their allegation that the whites here aren't interested in their welfare nonsensical, but that *they* are the ones totally uninterested in their own people's welfare. They are their own worst enemies! One hopes that their next step will be to cut out their hypocrisy.

6

WHILST THE BRITISH MAY NOT BE AWARE OF the hypocrisy of black people in England and their callousness towards each other, they have, however, been very much aware of these same faults among the blacks in Africa. The whole world, in fact, has been aware. For years the world has been puzzled, shocked and disgusted by the doings of the Africans to themselves—the terrible sufferings and bloodshed that have taken place in the numerous *coups d'état*; worse, the frightful results of the endless tribal wars. The world has witnessed Africans die in their tens of thousands, and recently in Biafra by their millions (2,500,000 to be exact). The world has witnessed savage atrocities in these tribal wars—uncurbed massacres, crucifixions, mutilations, cannibalism, disembowelling of innocent men, pregnant women and children, plus other unutterable forms of torture. The world has seen some of the best examples of man's inhumanity to man. The Africans have shown their total apathy to the value of life. Yet, at the same time, these same barbarous Africans point and scream their protests at the 'inhuman' treatment by the whites of the blacks in South Africa and Rhodesia. Oh, how I would rather see the continuation of the racial discrimination in these two countries than any more of the horrific massacres my fellow Africans have carried out on themselves. I'm one of those prophets of doom already saying that the disintegration of Africa is remediless, and Africa is finished. Black and white opponents of mine have often reminded me that when the Romans first invaded Britain, they found the British the most barbaric and warlike beings they had yet seen. Today look at the British. . . . The same way Africa would soon overcome her obstacles, my opponents figured. That was a comforting theory. I pray my opponents are right. But I'm still dubious. Violence being a 'component' of the black man, the Africans will, as they have been doing for generations, surely continue to settle their differences with violence. All that Western civilisation has done to them is change their tastes in life. They now have a mad quest for political power and no longer for mere tribal positions, greed for money and no longer for cattle, love for guns and bullets and no longer for bows and arrows, etc. But as people, western civilisation has totally failed to change them. Tribalism still lives and reeks in most black African countries, and warfare still remains the deciding factor of everything. And by acquiring the white man's superior armaments, the Africans have merely acquired faster means of destroying themselves.

Why, for goodness sake, couldn't the white colonists have left my people to continue their own way of life? This was a great mistake on their part. Much as they regarded African culture as inferior to their own, it mattered not. There's no universal means of measuring cultures. What may be good for one race may not be good for another. The Africans were contented and naturally suited to their way of life. But it's too late now. The white man's civilisation has taken over in Africa and has damaged most of the Africans' customs and culture beyond repair. Most Africans are now too 'detribalised' to ever want to live again as they once used to. And at the same time to live like the whites is proving something beyond their ability: it seems that they must die in their efforts. Today, in 1972, the long-standing hostility between the Hutu and Tutsi tribes of Central

Africa's Burundi, has broken out into a bloody strife. And after only three months of fighting, eighty thousand people have been massacred.

How can one see any future for black Africa? Other thorny facts are glaring out. Africa fails to see that if she is to assume any sort of parity with other continents in the balance of economic power, she must draw more effectively on her most abundant resources—namely her manpower potential. And for the good of Africa's economic future, each one of her people must not only assume a totally functional role, but must do so as well as possible for the greater good of the community as a whole. That's by no means the case in black African countries. The people are too callous and self-centred, especially the western-trained politicians and civil servants—the very individuals you would have thought that the masses could look up to. They merely return home from Europe and develop a grossly inflated sense of their own importance, then become too busy making money for themselves to care for the welfare of their people. They are becoming a burgeoning, middle-class dead-weight in their societies, and their essential function is that of a parasite—expensive, debilitating and deadly. Their whole attitude is this: 'Well, I have suffered, and my sufferings are now over. It's now my turn to prosper.' Is there the faintest glimmer of the thought: 'Let me go and serve my people with my skill which I owe them.'? No. Indeed, they expect their people to owe them a living for the rest of their lives, because they are the 'valuable' products of the white man's training.

Take the doctors, for example. Their only haunts are the cities and large towns, where they try and live the posh life, have their own surgeries and charge hell for their services. How many of them, out of sheer humanity, venture towards the traditional villages or the dark recesses to supply or treat sick natives who have no means of reaching them? One in a thousand. *Rarely* have I heard of such acts by African doctors. It's always white doctors, nurses, missionaries and western organisations such as the Flying Doctor Service. Many white people wrongfully believe that the shortage of doctors in African countries explains why natives in the dark recesses receive insufficient medical attention; whereas, the truth of the matter, as I have gathered from whites who have served in the medical profession in various parts of Africa, is that the large towns have an abundance of western-trained African doctors who regard the idea of venturing near the dark recesses as being below their standard and dignity.

The most dangerous of these parasitic sophisticates are those educated at English public schools. The public school is no place for an African. During the controversy aroused by the publication of *Nigger at Eton*, so many white people asked me what a person like me was doing at Eton in the first place, adding that I should never have been sent there. I agreed with them. Because the idea of sending a foreign schoolboy to public school, let alone a black African one, with his special cultural circumstances, seems to suggest a curiously misplaced sense of values. English people themselves have questioned the usefulness of a public school education in present-day English society. It's absurd for anyone to suggest that it would meet the needs of an emerging African society. Traditionally, the public school's role has been to provide for an already chosen minority of this society a privileged education that equipped them to fulfil their role, predestined by birth, as the pillars of the ruling class and leaders of the establishment. As such the status of the public school probably reached its zenith during the era of the British Empire. At those times they produced the very people most needed to spread the word of British power and wisdom among the backward people whose lands the crown had already occupied.

As Britain's Empire role has shrunk with the passage of time, and as Britain's position in the balance of world political and economic power has drastically altered, so has the role and status of the traditional public school become more and more disused. The traditional public school product has become out of date. His relative value in an increasingly technocratic society compares badly with the more functional scholar generally produced by the grammar or comprehensive schools.

In Africa, the position of the public school product is even more far-fetched. Today, Africa is virtually a world-wide farmyard and provider of natural resources for the more highly skilled technological countries. If Africa wants people who will work for the community as a whole, then such people should be specifically educated to meet a practical need. It's difficult to see where Africans educated at English public schools would fit into such a scheme. Indeed, the evidence suggests that their role could, in terms of the overall aims of Africa, be essentially counter-productive. As I've stated, they're the typical, self-important parasites who have an expectation of life that an African society could never hope to meet. From Africa's stand-point, it would be better that men of power emerged who, with sufficient vision, would forever ban this absurd practice of wealthy Africans having their children educated at English public schools. It's a practice that drains the life-blood and usefulness of those very people who might one day become our natural leaders, as it warps whatever potential they may have. And of course, their grandchildren will catch their diseases, and the left-over for the masses will always be poverty. And so bribery and corruption will continue to exist. From all this, one can only be left with a feeling of gloom regarding the possibility of any development in Africa's manpower potential.

One other major defect is holding Africa back: there is no long-term planning in anything the African does. His only interest is what life has to offer *today*. Get as much wealth and status as possible and let time take its course. *Que sera, sera*! This is the African's mentality. How can he improve himself? How can he develop his country for the future Africans? What does the future hold for his country? These important questions don't come into the mind of the self-interested African. Take as an ideal example the question of independence for the African states. All that one saw in the Africans was the overwhelming thrill that they were now to govern themselves. Their bag of nourishing thoughts was totally absent of any questions like: How would they govern their states? Would they have a capitalist state? Socialist? What? There was no aim of any sort. All that mattered to them was that as from now they were their own masters.

Then there is the question of creativity of the Africans. Apart from Art, there has been no sign of any spontaneous creativity by the Africans. The African is quite happy to sit on his backside and make do with the materials supplied to him by the white man. To try and make his own invention is something he'll not even dream about in a thousand years.

I suppose the Africans' failure to plan in advance finds its explanation in that their way of life before the colonial days was such that any long-term planning was unneeded. They had nothing really to plan or aim for, since theirs was a simple, uninhibited life in which their only study was the spiritual world. In addition, they were gullible to the extent that they knew nothing whatsoever of the world beyond their forests and their deltas. The whites, however, were bound to travel and plan ahead all the time to develop the zenith of their industrial achievements. This was important if they were to survive in their cold western climate. However, the fact that the Africans *still* fail to plan in the long-term is yet another example of how western civilisation has failed to change them as people. From a very reliable source, I learnt that a Russian diplomat had told an African counterpart: 'By the time you Africans reach the stage of the white man today, we shall be living on the moon.' I don't doubt that possibility at all. And when I summon the courage to look into the future, I see nothing but doubt and discontent among the Africans, and bloodshed after endless bloodshed—worse than we have yet seen.

I've been *violently* opposed to the suggestion of black freedom and majority rule in Rhodesia, with the stark knowledge that only chaos would be the result: the same chaos that the world has witnessed in other parts of black Africa, with flagrant abuse of power, bribery and corruption helping to invite bloodshed. I've often prayed that if ever the world should see black freedom and majority rule in Rhodesia, the white Rhodesians would have taught the Africans a few major lessons that the white colonists failed to do to the other African countries before leaving. The Africans should be made to realise that they're no longer living life as they used to before the arrival of the white man. Theirs is now western civilisation, a world of politics, of economic and technological developments. If they are to adapt fully to the requirements of western civilisation, they must rid themselves of certain characteristics that were, understandably, part of their own culture. For the whites in Rhodesia merely to show the blacks how the job is done isn't enough. It should be impressed upon them that only by long-term planning can they have any hope of progressing. They should be made to understand that to settle their differences, it would be safer and far more effective to have a round-the-table-confrontation and try to reach a rational, reasoned understanding: not brutal, inhuman and meaningless attacks on their own fellow men. In addition, the Africans should be taught to regard their jobs as sacred and take pride in them—not use them merely for their own benefit and to hurt people. By that I mean bribery, corruption and the misuse of power.

I think the whites in Rhodesia would have great difficulty impressing these essentials upon the Africans. It would take a long time if ever they did succeed. Violence, for instance, as I explained, is in the black man's blood; to get him to refrain from using it would be a difficult matter. The same surely applies to the question of bribery. The Africans don't have the feeling of the white man that bribery is base. For generations it has been like a game for them. In traditional African villages, for example, natives with the most beautiful daughters who offered their daughters' services as the Chief's servants were given responsible positions in the tribes; natives who offered the most precious gifts got the most attractive women to marry. Today this practice of giving and taking bribes still flourishes in nearly all branches of occupations all over black Africa, and all it means is that the most selfish, dishonest and greedy men infiltrate the key positions. For instance, the judges —most of whom allow themselves to be bought by political parties and do justice according to the wishes of their parties; ministers, who bribe to win electors, who demand a ten per cent cut from firms before awarding them contracts to undertake government constructions; politicians—whose idea of free and fair elections is to hire thugs to engage in the destruction of life and property.

The Africans in Rhodesia should be made to appreciate that violence and bribery may have been suited to their own culture many years ago, but today, in this modern world of politics, they only create complications. A number of black and white Rhodesians I've known informed me that whilst the world has a blazing awareness of the black and white palaver in Rhodesia, little is it known that bribery is the order of the day among the blacks themselves. The black police, for instance, misuse their powers and victimise their own people. Apparently, they expect to be given the fear and respect that the whites demand of the blacks.

So I can imagine that it would prove a lengthy process for the whites in Rhodesia to make the Africans see the dangers of displaying some of their cultural habits in western civilisation. I'd much rather it took a long time than the Africans be given the freedom to get at each others' throats. It would be the height of stupidity on the part of the white Rhodesians if they succumbed to the pressures of black Africa and the rest of the world and gave the Africans majority rule without their being ready for it. For such an action, they would be responsible for the hardships that the Africans would suffer at their own hands.

Much as these are my wishes, I do, at the same time, remain resentful that the whites should carry out their ideals of separate developments with antipathy and harshness towards the Africans. Personally, I'm slightly inclined to oppose the idea of racial integration and favour 'apartheid', and I'll explain why later. But I feel that 'apartheid' should be practised *only* in the company of mutual help, benevolence and respect between the races. The last two factors have not been the case in Rhodesia— what with the whites placing degrading restrictions on the blacks and confining them to the worst living quarters. And when one bears in mind that Rhodesia is, in fact, a black country, this cruel form of 'apartheid' is all the more distressing. I invert the word 'apartheid' because it has a different meaning from what the world believes. In *My People*, Credo Mutwa's book on the oral traditions of Southern Africa, he writes: 'The world has equated this word with discrimination, but in fact it means almost the opposite. To discriminate is to distinguish between two things and decide which of them is best. Apartheid is to distinguish *without* deciding which is best. Apartheid is a law of nature. . . .' Well, there can certainly be no denying that the whites are better than the blacks in this technological world, and as I have explained, it's only *fitting* that they should remain in control in Rhodesia in the meantime—for the good of the Africans. But it is wrong that they should allow apartheid and petty cruelty to run concurrently. If their unfair discrimination is not ended, all one can see in the future is bloodshed between the two races.

The same no doubt applies in South Africa. I needn't express my thoughts of the whites in South Africa—the world's worst practitioners of discrimination towards the blacks. But again what's so painful is that there's no solidarity among the Africans there. Credo Mutwa says in *My People* that crime flourishes in the black townships around Johannesburg and the people live in fear of murderers who have carried out scores of butcheries upon whole families. And as well as the dishonesty of many Bantu officials, 'the selfishness of the rich Bantu, who never gives anything even to Bantu charities, Bantu hospitals, old people's homes or children's feeding schemes, is a byword throughout South Africa. . . .'

Much as I'm resentful at the racial discrimination in Rhodesia and South Africa, I feel very little sympathy for the blacks there, as it's quite clear that they also thrive on making life hard for themselves and aren't prepared to help one another. It's very discomforting to have to confess that should they be in power today in Rhodesia and South Africa, they would be experiencing hardship such as would make the white man's present cruelty against them seem blessedly insignificant.

So again, as with the blacks in England, I also maintain that those in Africa are their own worst enemies, and should first sort themselves out before turning to rave at South Africa and Rhodesia. Bitter as they are at the racial practices in both countries, I believe that if the discrimination were to end there, the black African nations would suffer from acute unhappiness; for they would then have no excuse whatever for failing to be up to scratch themselves. So really, as well as hating apartheid, they're loving every second of it.

Whenever you hear an African in England complaining about the white man's injustices against his people, and you ask for his comments on the injustices his own people in Africa carry out on themselves, he'll always blame the white man; in no way are his people responsible. Here's a typical example of this. At Speakers' Corner one afternoon, a small group of noisy blacks were avidly reminding themselves that: 'We blacks are all the same; Americans, Africans, West Indies—we're all brothers. We all have the same cause. The white man is our enemy....' An Asian listener confronted the chief spokesman and with an air of patient courtesy, pointed out: 'It's all very well to say that you're all brothers, my friend. What about the time when Ghana threw out the Nigerians from the country? Where is the brotherhood in that . . . ?'

Before the chief spokesman could answer, this small, pot-bellied African cut in, and with a kind of theatrical declamation said: 'Ah!—but you see, wherever you get trouble between a black man and a black man, the white man's influence is dangling.'

'Ride on, Brother!' the other blacks backed him, nodding in agreement.

All seemed satisfied with Pot-Belly's answer. I didn't think it revealed where the brotherhood was in Africans ousting fellow Africans from their country. Rather than an honest concession that there was no brotherhood at all, Pot-Belly evaded the question and tried to justify the Ghanaians' action by inferring that but for the white man, the matter would never have occurred.

It's disturbing that most Africans here will always volunteer this invalid excuse for the faults of their people in Africa. It's fundamental self-deceit on their part to think they don't make mistakes themselves. The Africans themselves are responsible for their problems, and the same goes for the blacks here. It's high time that the black man burst out of that sweater of self-deceit already straining at the seams, and came to the reality that he is human, and that he can and does err. He has many faults, and there can be no hope of his curing them if he begins by denying their existence. It will do him no good to lie to himself, however bitter the truth may be.

Ask any black man to explain how the whites are responsible for the Africans' endless warfare between themselves, and there's only one answer he'll give you: That until the whites came to Africa, Africa was just one great expanse. The whites, on their arrival, drew up boundaries—to which they allotted the tribes. They divided up the tribes in each boundary, teaching them to hate and look down upon one another as being inferior. This would be in the best interest of the whites after their departure from Africa. The tribes would inevitably be up in arms against each other, weakening themselves—thus rendering themselves easy victims for exploitation. That's how the situation stands today. The whites mediate as the peace-making philanthropists and supervise an economic settlement—out of which they're left with more windfall for their balance of payments.

I've had no cause whatever to doubt that the whites did exploit the Africans in this way, but I refuse to accept that they intentionally planned that the Africans should fight among themselves so that they would become easily exploitable. That allegation implies that before the whites arrived there had always been peace and quiet in Africa. Of course, this wasn't so. The tribes had always been at each others' throats even before the arrival of the white explorers in the fifteenth century. The ownership of land was always determined by warfare: one tribe was always attacking the other and making use of the prisoners as slaves. It was the white slave-traders who arrived in the eighteenth century who exploited the situation. They merely waited in their boats by the seashore while the warriors from tribes, to whose chiefs the slave-traders had paid goods such as rum, trinkets, muskets and gay cloths in return for slaves, travelled through mile after mile of deep forest to raid other tribes and capture hundreds of fellow blacks, for whom the American plantations were howling like starving wolves. The next white people to arrive in Africa were the colonists. Once they had subdued the blacks and kept them in subservience, Africa suffered no further tribal wars during their presence. Once they left, it was back to square one for the tribes. . . .

I can't see, then, that black people here are at all justified in blaming the white man for the fighting in Africa, as this has been the sport of our people for decades. The white man's major crime was to deprive the Africans of their way of life in the first place; more so for giving in to the Africans' agitation for independence—knowing they weren't ready for it. There's certainly no reason to forgive the white man for giving them independence. There's even less reason to forgive the Africans in England for refusing to recognise their people's own faults.

My fellow men should also bear in mind that the atrocities

the white slave-traders committed against our people wouldn't have happened but for the Africans themselves. It was they who sold the slaves to the whites and as such are to blame for the agonies their brothers suffered as a result. This is one major factor my fellow men always seem to forget whenever they voice their hatred against the white slave-masters. Though they now spit with disgust on the idea of slavery, and will always instinctively remember it as having been the white man's usage on their own people, they shouldn't at the same time forget that slavery had been a common African practice before the arrival of the slave-traders. Even *today*, in 1972, it's still practised in Sudan, Timbuktu and in Nigeria: men, women and children are still being bought and sold for slave-work. Yes, black people are worse practitioners of slavery than the whites. They're also worse offenders of the other crimes they accuse the white man of practising against them.

As with the blacks in England, other major flaws in the characteristics of those in Africa which they must learn to get rid of are actions which depict them as being fundamentally stupid souls: actions that one can only frown upon and as a result have a low rating of Africans in general. What hurts most is that the stupid acts we normally hear about are committed by the very people you would have expected to show a much higher degree of intelligence.

For instance, a well-known western-trained African leader was expecting an important visit from a fellow countryman for talks on official matters. The guest arrived at the Presidential residence, was ushered into the President's office, and beheld a sight he considered the height of disgrace. The President's table was totally devoid of any official papers; and there was the President himself—lazily reclining in his chair with his feet on the table, listening to pop-music. And this, thought the guest later, was the mentality of a man expected to have the intelligence and competency to run a nation. You may think that incident petty; but since that President came to power, his country has, until today, been in rubble.

The other examples in my mind are more serious than that one. In early 1967, for instance, a major event took place in the former Belgian Congo. It was televised and hit the headlines of the British press. I've yet to overcome the shame I experienced at watching the Africans make the world wonder if they carried their brains elsewhere than in their heads. Here's a brief background to the facts that led to the event. The presence of the wealthy Belgians in the Congo had long been an unwanted one, as it was felt they were sabotaging the country's economy. This was evident from the massacres of Belgian citizens by Africans in the early and later stages of the 1960s. One influential African who had been friendly towards the Belgians, if you remember, was the late President Moise Tshombe: the same man who, in 1960, made an abortive attempt to separate the Congolese province Katanga as a national entity of its own, proclaiming himself its President. After the bloody civil war that ended in the recapture of Katanga, a settlement was reached—out of which Tshombe became Premier of the whole country in 1963 for three years before being overthrown and going in exile to Europe. In stepped Belgian Colonel Schramme. This elderly mercenary fighter was suitably nicknamed 'Black Jack': as a small boy, he had watched his own parents shot dead by Africans, and it was subsequently reported that he vowed to kill as many blacks as he could. However, Schramme tried to restore the deposed Tshombe, as it would be in the interests of Belgian businessmen living in Katanga that he returned to power. This was where the main facts of the humiliating events I mentioned begin to unwind themselves.

The pathetic size of Schramme's army was a little over a hundred men—mostly white South African mercenary recruits, and a handful of loyal black supporters of Tshombe who voluntarily offered to fight free of charge. Schramme's armaments consisted of just one tank and rifles for his men. Bearing in mind the fact that the Congolese army numbered 38,000 men, one must surely see Schramme as a real lunatic if he genuinely believed he could take Katanga without being blasted into orbit in the attempt. He was, however, determined to try and achieve his objective—regardless. But for America he may well have succeeded. On his route to Katanga lay Bukavu, a big, densely-populated town. The television showed a scene of pandemonium and uncontrolled panic among Bukavu's inhabitants at the seemingly imminent bloodshed that would take place between Schramme and the troops of the Congolese army stationed there to engage Schramme. The television showed the inhabitants fleeing like jackals with their belongings, leaving the one thousand troops to face the music. One thousand troops!— with all the necessary arms and defensive positions to engage and rout Schramme's Soldiers of Fortune. Schramme's approach into Bukavu—down a road running into the hills—made him a sitting target. Yet, even before he was seen or heard, the Congolese troops started to get cold feet. Panic seized them too. They piled their weapons together on the ground ready to leave them and flee. And moments later, when the unseen enemy were finally heard, they took to their heels in consternation—allowing the triumphant mercenaries to walk in and occupy the ghost town. The television showed these details. I was in London at the time, on holiday from Eton. I watched this shameful display of cowardice in the little sitting-room of my host's semi-detached residence. A number of his African colleagues from the embassy were present. I remember that at the end of the film a pregnant silence invaded the room; it seemed to last nine months, before the verbal barrage from the viewers opened up. The whites were so biased against Africans, they complained; always keen and prompt to belittle the Africans but rarely eager to recognise or show their merits. Nobody raised a word to condemn the Africans for their disgraceful act. I remained silent, trying to fathom how such an action could possibly be forgiven. It seemed unbelievable that Schramme struck terror into an army ten times greater for no other reason than that his men were white. And why the Africans decided to leave their weapons at his disposal before their withdrawal was another puzzle I couldn't put together. My embarrassment intensified after I returned to Eton. For three weeks Schramme spent a 'peaceful vacation' in Bukavu. The Congo's 38,000 troops were powerless against his hundred men. Powerless! The next thing you knew was that the country's President, General Mobutu, was crying for American help to fight Schramme. America, which had close links with the Congo, quelled Mobutu's fear by sending in fighters to drive Schramme out. That an army of 38,000 men couldn't oust a hundred sparsely-armed intruders from their own territory without foreign aid was simply too pathetic for words. It makes you wonder why the Congo had an army at all.

Most disturbing of all is that that incident throws a complete shadow of doubt on one popular belief held by so many blacks in this country: that if equipped with the necessary amount of weapons and training, any black African country would be a match for South Africa or Rhodesia, and that apartheid wouldn't be throbbing with as much arrogance as it's throbbing today. You simply have to laugh at that and keep laughing. Totally overlooking the fact that the Africans' greatest problem is first to sort themselves out, the white man, as was evident in the Congo, still has this psychological power over the Africans. And I doubt whether any African country, equipped with all the requirements to deal with South Africa or Rhodesia, would have the stomach even to contemplate the idea, let alone attempt it. Nor am I too keen to believe that all the black African countries combined would summon the courage to try. They've yet to break down that psychological barrier in their minds before they could fearlessly look the whites in Southern Africa in the eye. They must also learn to show far more competence than they've been doing so far. You may not believe this, but at the end of 1966, as the Nigeria/Biafra civil war was brewing, I put these anxious questions to an older relation of mine during the holidays: 'Are you sure our chaps will have the knowledge to operate their weapons? Do you reckon they'll operate them with enough competence to hit the Nigerian planes and ships?' Perhaps rather juvenile questions for a boy nearing sixteen years of age, admittedly, but I asked them in all seriousness. My relation, fully aware of my low opinion of black people, replied in a nondescript sort of tone: 'Well, one can only hope so; otherwise that's our lot.' So inefficient and stupid did I regard Africans, that those questions really worried me.

The Nigerian war did, in fact, see frightfully stupid actions. One white South African mercenary employed to train the Nigerian pilots was so unimpressed that in an interview with western journalists he slated the Nigerians as being the most unteachable bunch of bungling idiots he had come across. With the kind of horrors the Nigerians were constantly perpetrating, he could hardly be blamed. For example, one of the pilots he trained was sent on a bombing mission to Biafra. Instead, he flew five hundred miles the opposite way, ended up in Dahomey —another country—and crashed. As another example, on several of the occasions that the South African pilot flew

Dakota DC3s on bombing missions to Biafra, the Nigerians
on board responsible for de-fusing and dropping the bombs
over the target zone, kept de-fusing them while the plane was
still droning over Nigerian territory, with the result that they
had no alternative but to release the bombs on their own territory—or disintegrate the entire plane.

Yes, the sort of thoughtless actions that black Africa could
well do without if she is one day to come into confrontation
with nuclear-armed South Africa. It's essential that the Africans
learn to recognise the importance of their brains in a time of
war.

These acts of stupidity may well be all in the past, but the
times of their occurrence don't date back far (within the last
five years), and it's disturbing to behold glaring signs which
suggest that the Africans propose to continue their stupid ways.
For instance, not long ago I picked up a copy of the London
Evening News. In the 'Our World Tonight' page, the headline
read: 'City of "ear for an ear" justice', under which was a large
picture of a gleeful African waiting with a large crowd at a
market square to witness the punishment of six condemned
criminals. The story is best left in the words of the report:

*'These men are waiting for justice—Central African Republic style.
Soon one of their ears will be cut off—for being a thief. All in full public
view in the Republic's capital, Bangai. The punishments were ordered by
President General Jean Bedel Bokassa who demanded "most severe"
punishments for thieves. Special Army detachments, headed by the
General carry out the barbaric punishments. Thieves lose one ear for the
first offence, the other for the second and their right hand the third time.
Some are badly wounded—some die. This is justice—Central Africa,*
1972.

And, in addition to that, President Bokassa made further
world headlines by his reaction to the condemnation of his

unnecessarily cruel justice by the Secretary-General of the United Nations, Austrian Dr Kurt Waldheim. 'Pimp! Imperialist! Colonialist!' said President Bokassa. This is the mentality of an African President, 1972.

The greatest tragedy is that most black African leaders have the same kind of low mentality as President Bokassa, and this is why we make such slow progress. It's worrying to sit down and wonder just how many more 'Bokassas' the future will present as African leaders. All I can do is make one final appeal to my fellow Africans that as long as they continue to act like stupid children, the world will treat them as such. And they cannot in any way be justified in calling the white man a racialist or imperialist when he inevitably expresses disgust at the atrocities they commit and is caused to think poorly of them.

I'd like to end the topic by drawing your attention to the fact that President Bokassa, with his remarks to Dr Waldheim, displayed a characteristic of the black man today. That he would not recognise the iniquity of his so-called justice was evidence that, like most of his black brothers in the world, he can't face reality. And I must stress: nothing could be more pathetic than a man deliberately blinding himself to the bright lights of reality. Nothing could be more disconsolate than a man who, on being presented with concrete evidence of something, insists with stubborn conviction that the evidence is false. It's as absurd as showing a man a gleaming blue ocean in the distance, while he insists that the ocean is not there. How will you ever teach such a man anything? Such a man is the black man today.

7

WHEN I OBSERVE THE RACIAL TENSION IN THE
world today, one mystifying question I've never stopped asking
myself is why it appears that only *white* prejudice matters? Why
do *both* the black and white races put such a great emphasis on
the white man's prejudicial practices, as if it's the most grave
and dangerous kind that exists? Sure enough, the white man
has a long record of persecution of the blacks to answer for. But
this was mostly in the past, and is no just reason why, in this
present day and age, colour prejudice by the whites should be
hotly attacked wherever it pokes out its ugly nose, whilst nothing is said about tribalism or racialism in black Africa. Once
again we must be realistic. Tribalism, nationalism and even
racial prejudice stink in black African countries to such an extent as to make their western counterparts seem trivial. Although
I've already looked at the controversy surrounding Enoch
Powell's race speeches in my first chapter, there are a few
unstated factors of some importance which we should observe.
When Powell points out the dangers of immigration and merely
suggests that the black immigrants should be given financial
backing by the British government to return home *voluntarily*,
a tumult reverberates through the world and he's branded a
racialist monster. Yet when Ghana started repatriation of the
Nigerians in 1969, the world held its peace. When the Hausas of
Northern Nigeria drove out the million Ibos living there and
slaughtered 33,000, the world looked the other way. When

Kenya started repatriation of Asians, the world had no comment to make. Furthermore when, in the early and later stages of the 60s the unwanted Belgians were raped, tortured and massacred in the Congo and forcibly sent home, the reaction of the world was, comparatively, very slight. Why were the Africans not condemned and denounced by the world as racists or tribalists? When they order out their aliens at spearpoint why do they escape the world's indignation whilst Powell is hated simply for suggesting voluntary repatriation? How is he so different that he alone must be branded a racialist? Why does black prejudice not count?

Let's face it, tribalism, for instance, is so bad in Africa that Africans themselves are unsafe in their own environment. It'd by unrealistic for any black man (or white man for that matter) to try and deny that the Africans have been doing themselves far greater harm than ever the whites did to them. And for this reason, reality forces us to concede that a black African would be much safer in any part of the western world than in any part of black Africa—let alone his own particular environment. In fact, we can go further than that and positively maintain that all the blacks outside Africa—the West Indians, the Afro-Americans, the lot—would be far more secure where they are now than they would be in any part of black Africa. If one day we were to see an influx of jubilant Afro-Americans and West Indians into Africa, supposedly returning home to 'black brothers', it wouldn't be long before we witnessed that same file of human fodder in a mass exodus from Africa, returning in humiliation to their 'white masters'—almost like centuries ago. To the black Africans they wouldn't be 'brothers', but unwanted aliens coming to sabotage their countries' economy. The popular 'peace and love, brother' chant that re-echoes throughout the black communities in America and

England has absolutely no meaning to the Africans in Africa. Infuriating is the fact that the blacks in the western world are fully aware of this but turn a blind eye and continue to announce stubbornly that the whites are the black man's burden. As I explained, the black man has yet to learn to face reality.

It's strange, however, that the white race itself should be particularly obsessed with its own racial prejudices, knowing full well that black Africa is the homestead of prejudice in all the worst conceivable forms. Why doesn't it also concentrate its anger and anxiety on the Africans, knowing that they are a greater danger to themselves than the whites have ever been to them? There are two reasons I strongly believe why the white nations feel the need to look the other way and say nothing. One, out of guilt and shame for their long record of persecution of the blacks; two, because they crave economic and diplomatic links with Africa by maintaining a good relationship with her. So what, in effect, results is that by overlooking tribalism and racialism in black Africa, the white man is successfully making the Africans believe that their prejudicial practices are harmless and excusable, and that only white prejudice is vile. The white man is at great fault here. Racial or tribal prejudice is wrong when carried out either by blacks or whites. The African nations should be made to appreciate this. The white man, by encouraging the Africans to believe their prejudicial practices are admissible, is more or less encouraging them to continue their tribal wars and inflict infinitely greater harm on themselves. Pressures of world opinion should be severely applied to the Africans when they engage each other in warfare. And, if the world is ready to condemn Enoch Powell, it should also condemn the Africans when they practise their form of 'Powellism'. There can be no doubting that African countries would yield to world pressure with considerable ease, since they are essentially dependent on the outside world for financial and technical assistance.

Of course, England, Master of Patience, is the only white country where black prejudice is allowed to function with the utmost arrogance, whilst white prejudice is always attacked fiercely—by both races. The British newspapers are always keen to blaze any act of white racialism across their pages, and blacks are equally eager to condemn it. But blacks' grievances against white girls, the racially-insulting language used by underground black magazines, by black orators at Speakers' Corner, etc. are all, it seems, beyond notice. I might take this convenient opportunity to mention that among the white orators at Speakers' Corner, you'll never see one expressing racial feelings against black people. Should that happen, the possibility of the Battle of Speakers' Corner presenting itself surely wouldn't be remote. And, of course, the blacks would make the initial assault on the whites. Again the point is crystal clear: *only* blacks can exhibit their prejudice without any condemnation. So, having travelled through centuries riding the myth that the blacks can do no good, the Englishman, it seems, has now started to pedal a new myth that they can't do anything wrong. The British would do well to destroy this myth. The longer this myth lives, the greater the possibility of a race war in Britain. And though there can be no doubting that the British would have no problem in quelling any uprising by the blacks at the moment, I wouldn't be too eager to stake that such would be the case if the government insists on prolonging its guest treatment towards my impossible fellow men. You see, it's all very well for the nose-in-the-air aristocrats to sit in their distinguished ranks and flatter themselves that Britain is more tolerant towards the blacks than any other country in the world; the Leaders of the Establishment may well boast that the blacks here have never had it so good. But these learned philanthropists seem to overlook the fact that most of my fellow men are crime incarnates who have no sense of gratitude; they deny that there's *nothing* they could do for black people that would satisfy them. The more acts of goodness the government displayed towards the blacks, the more the blacks would scream for more, more and more! As I've stated, they'd merely take everything for granted and still maintain their dislike for the white man, creating a rumpus at the slightest thing that upset them—whilst they themselves were allowed to exhibit their prejudice at will. Whilst Britain has learnt to show tolerance and understanding towards them, she has yet to learn the one lesson that really matters: that it doesn't pay to be *soft*! Britain has been displaying softness and my fellow men are taking advantage of this. Whilst she has no apparent intention of repatriating them, she seems to turn a blind eye to the fact that the future will produce blacks, blacks and more blacks. . . . Black babies are being born at a rapid rate. And let's make no mistake about it, most of the future blacks in England will be brought up by their relations to dislike white people. Their ears will be filled with the usual bla, bla about the white man's criminal record. They may not know many details, but they'll know the general picture. I've encountered a number of black youths who were born and brought up here, and who've had dislike for the whites instilled in them by their fellow men. So what then? Well, as the passing of time expands the population of my resentful fellow men, *more* and *more* blacks will grow up believing the myth that only *they* can show their prejudice against white people, whereas the reverse is deplorable and is forbidden. And of course the British government will turn a blind eye to this growing population and continue to play the role of admirable gentlemen by showing patience and softness.

Consequently, it'll reach the stage when that patience will run out, owing to excess of my fellow men's insane desire to have everything their own way. And when the government finally slams down the brakes and for once decides to turn a deaf ear to my fellow men's hue and cry, we'll see the racial tension in England boil as it has never boiled before. The only drawback would be that the government would have chosen the wrong moment to lose its patience. The population of the black would have increased greatly, making them more formidable opponents. And all this because of the government's petty desire to live down its people's criminal record against the blacks by setting itself up as the world's most tolerant gentlemen.

This may all sound like vague, philosophical conjecture, but this is what I fear will be the situation if the government carries on its soft attitude. Sooner or later the government will have to make a firm stand, and there's no reason why it can't do so now. It has done all that's necessary to bring harmony between the races. Quite apart from the Race Relations Board, Race Relations Act and Institute of Race Relations, there's the Community Relations Commission with its local branches throughout the country; and there's the House of Commons Select Committee composed of a dozen MPs, whose function it is to study the housing conditions of non-white immigrants, investigate relations in multi-racial occupations and hear the views of immigrant leaders. It would be fair to say that the whites in England have done their best to make up for their criminal record against the blacks. But for the government also to insist on carrying on its 'unique' display of patience towards my fellow men simply makes no sense at all, as only racial bloodshed could be the ultimate result. And who wants that?

The government could begin by making it clear to my fellow

men that racial prejudice by themselves won't be tolerated either. As a first gesture, the government could prohibit any further speeches at Speakers' Corner deliberately designed to create violent antagonism between racial groups, and veto the successful attempts of Black Power magazines to heighten the racial tension. And as for the Press, they should be sternly warned to refrain from their deliberate attempts to put a racial interpretation on matters simply because individuals of different race or colour are involved, when such may not have been the original basis: it would be okay, of course, if a matter was unquestionably a case of racialism.

The government's next step should be to consider seriously repatriating those black immigrants who propose to live here permanently. Black students could be allowed to remain on condition that they returned home to their motherlands to be of some use after completing their studies. Black people should be the first aliens to be repatriated. This wouldn't be racialism, it would be common sense. As to why blacks in particular should be repatriated, let's completely overlook some of the reasons I've already mentioned—such as their countries need them, that most of them are disgracing the black race by voluntarily being exploited here, that their population here is too great. Let's forget these and look at two other more compelling explanations—both of which are incorporated in the one chief reason that it's impossible to effect a good relationship between the black and white races in England. First of all, my fellow men don't want friendship with white people, and so it makes no sense that they should continue to live in a country with whose inhabitants they don't want friendship—only hostility. As a result hostility is what they've got, and as time goes on the mutual mistrust and doubt will simply grow—until race war takes over. Secondly, even assuming that both races were eager for a friendly relationship, it would still be impossible. Each has totally different standards of morality. You've got a situation where the blacks come to England and bring all their natural habits with them—habits which, by white standards, are quite sickening and intolerable. You have a situation where what's acceptable to the people of one culture isn't acceptable to the people of another. So to expect them to live side by side in brotherhood is as absurd as expecting the sun to rise in the west. You've got the black man—violent, sensitive, ill-humoured, noisy who will unconsciously spit in the street, and you've got the white man—who is completely the opposite. So there stands the impossible situation. With their different cultures, different moral standards, the blacks, in the wake of their vast influx into this country are, in fact, making an enormous impact on the old English way of life. They've taken over whole streets in various parts of England, and, consequently, ghettoes have appeared where none ever existed before—evidence, again, of blacks' comparatively dirty existence. Naturally, the English people resent this with increasing despair and frustration. It's not so much that they hate the blacks, but simply that they are proud people who deplore the idea of their way of life being changed by a race of people with a totally different background, mentality and moral standards, all of which they consider to be inferior to their own. It seems, however, that all they can do is force a smile and bear it, and learn to accept people of different creeds. They daren't voice their feelings for fear of being accused of racialism and consequently face legal repercussions. The only individuals who have any say in the matter are the politicians and civil servants, and the British masses must remain silent and pay for their mistakes. Whilst I would shake the British people by one hand for learning to live with people of a different creed, I would wave away my fellow men with the other hand for their simple, upright lack of consideration. They should refrain from exhibiting their habits in public. They should know that only by adapting themselves to the *status quo* in this country can they be accepted by her people and accorded the respect which they complain they don't get. But alas! My fellow men's only interest is to acquire the luxuries of western technology, but as people, proudly wish to remain their natural selves—wherever they may be living.

Thus the reasons why the black and white races in England will never live happily together. The only blacks who can integrate successfully in a white country are those like myself, who have had the best of both the black and white cultures, and can naturally adjust to the two different life styles. But such fortunate blacks, I regret to say, are the tiny, tiny minority.

The differing cultures and moral standards between blacks and whites are the reasons why I'm inclined to oppose the idea of racial integration. These are the only reasons; but for them, I wouldn't hold any views about the basic moralities between racial integration and segregation: either would be acceptable to me. However, as the situation stands today, it would be senseless to try to integrate the races, as it wouldn't work. Neither race would want to adapt to the other's ways. So it would seem that the only way to establish a good relationship would be to separate them. In countries like Rhodesia, South Africa and America—officially recognised as black and white countries—separate developments could work swimmingly— only, as I stated once, in the company of mutual help, bene- volence and respect between the races. In those countries both the blacks and the whites are enthusiastic about the idea of separate developments—certainly the blacks are. As Credo Mutwa says in *My People*: 'What the world fails to realise is that apartheid is what the Bantu want, from the Transkei up to Nigeria and Ghana. Apartheid is what we want and what we need—what we do not want is discrimination!' And as is well known, the same applies to the blacks in America.

But in England 'apartheid' can never work. Of course, the black immigrants want apartheid—which is evident by the fact that they prefer to settle more in racial groups than spread themselves around among the whites. But this will do no good to anybody. Firstly, because the blacks have no desire for friendship with the whites, and so the racial tension will continue to reek. Secondly, the British government will continue to regard segregation to be racialist and immoral and prefer the blacks to integrate with the whites. Thirdly, the white folks don't want their own country—the England they once knew and helped to build—to fade and give way to the alien blacks. As far as they are concerned let the blacks separate themselves elsewhere—not in England. So it's clear that the only way good relations can be effected between the black and white races in England is that my fellow men be neither integrated nor segregated, but repatriated. This is the hard truth, and if the government isn't prepared to face it, then it should be prepared to face the ugly possibility of racial war as the black population expands.

My views aren't in the least bit deflected by the argument I've heard so often that many blacks have every right to be here: that the British, at the end of the war, was short of manpower, so invited the West Indians to come and work, with promises of security and permanent livelihood in England. Sure, the British did invite the West Indians to come and be exploited and they willingly came. But at that time Britain was in need of them; now they are no longer needed, and their departure wouldn't be destructive to England's economic situation. Let's be realistic about this. Britain didn't mean that 'the entire West Indian population' should swarm her, leaving her like some overweighted bag at splitting point; nor could Britain have possibly anticipated that she would be suffering the dreadful racial tension breathing in her midst today. There are times when people have to break promises. So whatever promises Britain gave the West Indies, the time has finally come when, for the good of the blacks and the whites, those promises must be overlooked and the West Indians (whether or not they possess British passports) be resettled in their rightful places in the Caribbean. Sure, it might prove difficult getting the blacks to leave, but it might also prove impossible if the matter is allowed to rest too long. And, as the saying goes: 'Never put off till tomorrow what you can do today.'

Enoch Powell should be considered a precious gift from God to the British people. He has the courage to voice the opinions that most whites hold but daren't express. He has enough vision to see the dangers that lie ahead with black people and accordingly alert the nation. The only sadness is that he doesn't have a hope of ever becoming Prime Minister. The government could do well to heed his warnings and carry out his suggestion of financial backing to the blacks to return home.

That's another reason that blacks have volunteered for their presence here: that they can't afford to return home. In the case of most blacks, you'll find that this isn't really true. It's not that they can't afford it, but that they don't want to afford it. And they don't want to afford it because, in truth, Britain (not the British) is like heaven to them: they simply love this country. They know that no other country could offer such security (financial or otherwise)—least of all their own countries; and they know that no other country could be so tolerant and understanding as this one. If it was my fellow men's genuine wish to return home, they could easily do so. They could start to save money and make plans for their means of subsistence at home. Since Powell first started his speeches in 1967, they've had five years in which they could have economised and saved enough money to see them home—if, as I say, they genuinely wanted to return home. But no. To the blacks, money is for spending, so spend it they will—here and now. That's the black man for you. No direction of any sort, no interest in improving himself. So the suggestion that they want to go home but can't afford to is nonsense. Enoch Powell is wasting his breath by suggesting *voluntary* repatriation with the financial backing of five thousand *per capita*. My fellow men would never go voluntarily for such a sum—unless they were offered some exorbitant figure which the Government couldn't afford. THE ONLY WAY to bring about their departure would be to deport them. And let's not forget that any black country wouldn't waste time in deporting unwanted aliens.

To reduce and control the number of aliens crowding Britain, the government introduced a secure system for that purpose by its enactment of the 1971 Immigration Act. I've never forgotten the way that my fellow men, as was characteristic, displayed their stupidity by misrepresenting the simple terms of the Act when the idea was initially debated by the public early in 1971. Virtually bursting the ear-drums of the nation with their protests, they were considering demonstrations and industrial action in order to prevent the Act becoming law. Why? Because they saw it as being discriminatory towards future black immigrants and as imposing limitations on the freedom of those already here, when, in actual fact, the rights of all immigrants in the country and their dependents were in no way affected. My fellow men aroused unnecessary fear among themselves through their misrepresentation and hypersensitivity. For example, their interpretation of the Act's 'patrial' and 'non-patrial' clause was that it distinguished between black commonwealth immigrants and white ones, and that it was mostly whites who would be permitted to settle in Britain permanently. Whereas the truth of the matter was that the Act was merely differentiating between people with close ancestral ties with Britain (the patrials), and those without (the non-patrials)—which was perfectly reasonable. Of course it meant that whites mostly would be allowed to settle in Britain, since all the patrials are white. The Act stated that future non-patrial immigrants (black or white) coming for employment would be given cards of identity and a certain status with which they could register at certain intervals with the police, so that one could keep a record of their whereabouts. Though they weren't bound to carry their cards on them permanently, the police could ask to see them at any time: as long as the cards were at home or available, all was well. This was a sure way of checking that the owners weren't illegal immigrants or unregistered aliens. My fellow men simply had to get all the facts wrong. In their eyes *only* blacks would have to carry cards— including (as was not true) those already here: that they would be subjected to random police checks (again another falsehood). As far as they were concerned, the police would get new powers which they would surely use to persecute them (as if the police didn't already have enough powers which they could abuse). My fellow men showed a total disregard of the fact that European and American aliens working here have had to undergo the same system of registration for years, and the procedure has worked very well with them. But once it started to apply to commonwealth immigrants, my fellow men had to believe *they* were being racially discriminated against. Likewise as with the one-year probationary period clause of the Act, prohibiting future non-patrial immigrants (black or white) from automatic settlement here. My fellow men also overlooked that Americans and Europeans themselves have been undergoing this identical one-year probationary period, during which time they, too, must live and work in a specific area, and can only obtain an extension from the Home Office if their behaviour has been good. It's only reasonable that such conditions should be made by a government before it allows permanent settlement. Sooner or later, the British government had to put a curb on the great influx of aliens, and I think you'll have to agree that if the last privilege of automatic settlement should be given to anybody, it is only fitting that it be to those with close ancestral ties with Britain. By the way my fellow men carried out their unjustified protests, anyone would have thought that this government didn't have the right to choose who could and could not settle in its own country. As I said, my fellow men will always want things their own way. And this is what comes from the government's softness towards them. This Act was fair and sensible. To add the final piece to the immigration puzzle, the government's next immediate duty should be to start repatriating black people.

You may wonder why I don't set an example myself by going home. Certainly, it's my ultimate intention to return home to my own people and loved ones. But right now it isn't that simple. The chief reason is that at only twenty-one I'm still on the young side. My purpose in coming to England was to learn; and though my unsuccessful academic career is over, there's still a lot to be learnt. My only desire in life is to write—journalism and writing books being my fields, in both of which I don't have enough experience—an essential which must be taken care of. And as I'll always be writing in English, in no better place could I acquire the experience than in England—particularly in journalism. Things haven't been helped by my having to live off social security since my parents stopped supporting me. Because I consider it a bit undignified for one to live off social security, I've always felt deeply ashamed to be doing so myself. The only way I can redeem myself is to bear in mind constantly the fact that this is a stage most writers go through. Hopefully, I'll soon be on my own two feet again.

For these reasons I can't return home right now. However, despite the great security that Britain offers, my place is not here; nor do I like Britain enough to want to live here for good. Despite the ethnic instability in black Africa, I wouldn't run away from such an important challenge. It's the duty of every black man to return home and focus his every effort towards helping to stabilise his motherland in whatever way possible. So it will be in my case—hopefully, in the not too distant future.

8

SINCE I WAS TWENTY, I HAD ALWAYS LONGED
for the chance to publicise some of my feelings about black
people in England. Though this book was already being planned,
I was suffering so much from disillusionment at their behaviour
that I was longing to make known my views in articles to the
press. As it happened, I managed to fight off the temptation to
write any such exposé, deciding to save my views for this book.
However, quite unexpectedly, a series of golden opportunities
brought me face to face with the public, and make myself heard
I did. It all started early in March 1972, a few weeks before
publication of *Nigger at Eton*. I was invited along to discuss the
book and my experiences at Eton on television. Unfortunately
the five-minute 'live' programme was too brief to enable me to
give my fellow men the verbal going-over that I had intended,
and my Eton contemporaries my criticisms of them. The
nearest I came to it was at the end of the interview when I stated
that despite my unhappy experiences at the hands of the white
Etonians, I was, nonetheless, left in no doubt that the black
man was his own worst enemy in England. The interviewer cut
me short, as there was no time to elaborate. For this reason I
was invited back the following day to continue the discussion
with Louis Chase, a West Indian journalist who, I gathered
beforehand, felt very strongly about the so-called hardships the
blacks were suffering from white people. Though very excited
at the prospect of expressing my feelings on television, I still

felt confident. I spoke in loud, belligerent tones, as if voicing a very serious complaint. Asked by the same interviewer to give my reasons for my statement the previous day, I mentioned two of the examples stated in this book: my fellow men's hypocrisy—the fact that they exploited one another and weren't at all interested in each other's welfare. Whereupon, I discharged a series of other accusations. Briefly, I mentioned their lack of gratitude towards this country's amazing display of patience towards them; that they should return home, as they were being exploited here; that they were too violent and couldn't reason; that they brutalised white girls, were only interested in their bodies, and cared nothing should the girls become pregnant, since this was the treatment black girls had suffered during the slave-days. I declared that my fellow men were like animals—excessively noisy and dirty—my examples of the latter being that they urinated in the streets and in basins. I added that such was my disappointment with black people that, if given a choice, I'd prefer another four years of racialism at Eton than my present experiences with them. These statements sparked off an argument between Mr Chase and myself. No doubt, rather shocked by these outbursts from a fellow black man, he remained calm and disputed everything I said, labelling me an 'Afro-Saxon'. The amazed interviewer suggested that my views were the result of my Etonian indoctrination. Mr Chase agreed that that was undoubtedly the case. I disagreed. So in fact I supported Enoch Powell? asked the interviewer. Yes, was my prompt reply. Would *I* eventually return home? Certainly.

It was a fifteen-minute programme, after which we retired to the thronged guest-room for drinks. There I learnt that in the course of the programme a profusion of phone calls had been made by irate blacks with messages of outrage. Members of the

TV staff jested that I should watch my step and not turn round dark corners too quickly.

Satisfaction nourished my veins after that interview. I was pleased with my performance. I had now cleared my system of certain unpleasant feelings that had molested it for a long time. Mind you, I realised later on that I shouldn't have made such a sweeping generalisation by making it sound as if *all* blacks committed the stated horrors—in particular, this question of soiling the streets and basins. I was, in fact, thinking of the black mothers I had seen allow their kids to do it: and only on four instances did I witness black grown-ups (educated ones too) use the basins in their homes rather than the toilets. It did occur to me that this generalisation was unfair. Obviously, I had been too excited to realise that I was generalising.

On the night of the interview a black friend of mine went to a pub frequented by blacks, and overheard a group of Black Power youths vowing that should they ever get hold of 'that black Englishman', they'd have his head. My friend advised me to watch it, as they were really mean cats. I heeded his words, but made it clear that I wasn't worried. In a free, democratic country like this, one was entitled to one's own opinions; and as I was sincere in my beliefs, no strong-arm tactics could deflect them, prohibit my voicing them, or frighten me. Besides, I debated, surely blacks would realise that by beating me up for merely voicing opposing views, they'd be proving my point that they couldn't reason?

But prove my point they did. Judging from the events of the months that followed, I had obviously incurred the hatred of most blacks who had watched that programme. It was flattering to be approached by curious white folks now and again wanting to know if I was the Etonian fellow on television, some voicing agreement with my points, others not. Nonetheless, they were all amiable. That certainly can't be said of the countless blacks who accosted me in the streets. Each time a black figure came my way, my heart started a war-dance rhythm, and I was all set for trouble. I was usually assailed with the most foul-worded insults imaginable. On buses, trains, in shops as well as in the streets, they approached—men, women, girls and boys—and usually the world could hear every word they said. To start with their insults used to bore me, finally irritating me to a point at which I always uttered a sigh of annoyance. But usually I paid no heed. If I'd honestly thought I could make my abusers appreciate that their insults were proving damn all and would in no way change my views but merely re-affirm them, I would have tried; as it was, I knew I'd be better off saving my breath. A number of indignant West Indians who approached me in the streets announced that next time I should specify that it was we Africans who were the filthy blacks deserving of all my accusations—not West Indians. On such occasions I hastened to answer that as Britain's black population consisted mostly of West Indians, I was referring to West Indians in particular. I always left under an onslaught of oaths.

As you can imagine, I was involved in a number of red-hot arguments. 'I hope you realise what you've done,' was the grave remark of a very disappointed African friend. 'You've belittled your own people and many blacks will always hate you for that.' This label of traitor was the usual sort of charge being levelled at me during all my arguments. Amid the insults I always stood firm, admitting that it was unfair on my part to have generalised, but insisting that if most blacks continued to behave as they do today, so would I continue to belittle them. The arguments dragged on endlessly, without any hope of agreement between us. Many blacks, despite my assurances that such wasn't the case, remained convinced that I had

been bribed with money by television staff to make these
utterances: that they weren't my own feelings. They wouldn't
believe I meant every word I said, since I didn't express such
views in daily life. Nor would they accept the reasons I volunteered for this: simply that my attempts in the past to criticise
black people about race usually resulted in near punch-ups, so
I had packed up trying to oppose them in arguments on race,
preferring to keep my views mainly to myself.

Yes, as I expected, a number of old black friends abstained
from any further communication with me. But I wasn't at all
worried by all the hostility. I remained convinced that only by
being told the truth about himself could the black man overcome his faults.

Violence was the one thing I definitely expected to encounter.
I thanked my stars that I had left my former Lewisham home.
I met the landlord one afternoon and he told me that a number
of his incensed black friends, who had frequently seen me during my stay there, had come round specially to beat me up for
my statements on television.

My first encounter with violence came at Speakers' Corner
five days after the television interview. I must have been sur-
rounded by the biggest audience any orator could have ever
dreamed for, everybody keen to know what the big row was all
about. But nothing constructive could be said by anybody. My
attempts to reason with a few black characters were drowned
by insults and pushes from all sides. Nobody would give me a
chance to defend my views. Next moment, a big, unshaven
black youth in shabby attire was so mad that he started to
crowd me, and amid obscenities, roughly clutched my coat-
collar and began to push me through the crowd towards the
entrance of the park, announcing that he proposed to kill me
outside. The crowd looked on—longing of course for a good

punch-up. But no. I didn't want to disgrace myself by engaging in a senseless brawl. Breaking his hold, I shoved him back and warned that I didn't want to fight, and should a fight take place he'd be the cause of it. But he still crowded me, insisting that I should come outside the park with him. So I went towards the main entrance gate, where, by chance, two policemen happened to be standing. I made towards them. My assailant, seeing my intention, started to draw back. As I told the officers that I had been assaulted, he tried to lose himself in the crowd. But they spotted him, called him back. He was very defiant as they warned that he would be arrested if he tried to start any more fights. He insisted on walking off, only to be repeatedly pulled back by the police and forced to listen. Asked if I wished to take out a summons against him, I declined. The crowd dispersed, and that was that.

My second encounter with violence wasn't as easily taken care of as that one. It occurred some three weeks later at three o'clock one Sunday morning, following the end of the Saturday-night disco-dancing at an African club. I was still loitering around in the semi-dark dance-hall with some remaining guests shrieking away in conversation. One black sprawling obscenely in an armchair called me over and drowsily asked what point I was trying to make in my offensive statements on TV. I was never allowed to answer. A small, though bulky, African lounging on a settee near him intruded with loud, foul-mouthed criticisms of me. Once a friend, he had taken a firm dislike to me because of my TV remarks. He persisted with his insults, never allowing me to speak. Angrily I told him to shut his mouth before I did it for him. Whereupon, he sprang to his feet like an enraged lion, screaming: 'Touch me and I'll kill you!' Next moment his fist smashed into my mouth. I staggered back a few steps, spurting blood. Everything happened so quickly. I saw blackness, and in that blackness a million twinkling stars. I thought I would collapse, but somehow remained groggily on my feet. My assailant, restrained by several blacks, was breathing hard, hollering: 'I'll kill you!' His dynamic punch had effectively drained all the strength from my body, and I knew that I was in no fit state to fight. I went angrily upstairs, phoned the police. Within minutes six officers arrived from nearby Bow Street police station; but my assailant had very conveniently disappeared. I accompanied the officers to the station to file charges. I was told I had to find out my assailant's address, so that he could be summoned to appear in court. So Sunday afternoon saw me at Speakers' Corner, where he was a regular speaker. Two enormous lumps had risen on my lips where he had scored with his punch. I was bent on vengeance. I could no longer flatter myself that I had always been physically unscathed in fights. I wasn't keen on going to court; I had just called the police on the spur of the moment. I only wanted to get my assailant alone somewhere now that I was ready to fight and get my revenge. I simply wanted to heal my injured pride.

He was at Speakers' Corner. But when I confronted him he refused to speak, screaming: 'Go away!' On learning that I wanted his address, he called two police officers who, before an enormous curious crowd, took down and exchanged our addresses. To my amazement he announced that he would sue *me* for assault as well. My amazement was intensified when about six blacks who hadn't been present during the incident claimed they were his witnesses and had seen me hit him first. Of course, I furiously denied it. Anyway, I approached him later and told him that I wasn't really keen on going to court, but would be obliged if he would come quietly outside alone with me and finish the fight. But he wouldn't come without his friends, who mocked me, saying that I'd have to fight the lot of them. To cut a long story short, no fight took place. An African intermediary, very friendly to both of us, made him apologise to me, and I simply had to swallow that hurt pride and forget the matter. Although I was partly to blame for that punch by threatening to shut him up, his hostility towards me, nonetheless, is another example of the typical feeling of black people about my TV interview.

Since violence and bad temper bring out some of the animal instincts in man, I couldn't get over the fact that my fellow men, by their emotional reactions towards me in public under the observation of white people—couldn't see that they were acting like the animals I claimed they were. One white person commented on this—my friend, Gillian. She was a fleshy, gay redhead in her late teens. A great academic, she was violently opposed to most of my views about black people, and disliked my statements on TV. But then one incident made her start thinking.... She and I were strolling along a busy one-way street in New Cross one Sunday afternoon. Presently a tall, stout, black man confronted us. Middle-aged, he was a bearded, sly-looking character with a moustache. In a voice which had the husky vibrations of cello notes, he politely asked if I was the Etonian chap on TV. Receiving my answer, he thanked me and went. Five minutes later, as we walked along a quiet lane of semi-detached houses, a dark Rover car with two black passengers drew up alongside. At the wheel was our friend again. He did all the talking.

'It's me again,' he excused himself. 'I want to take up something with you even though you might tell me to get lost.' Gillian and I stopped. 'You made a few remarks on television—'

Sighing with boredom, I told him to get lost and we resumed walking. Then it happened.

'No, I won't get lost!' he screamed viciously, keeping up with our pace. 'You fucking well listen to me.' He was like a wild-cat. 'You went on television condemning blacks for going around with white girls, and yet there you are doing exactly the same thing yourself. You fucking hypocrite!' Whereupon he started firing obscenities, which must have been heard all over the neighbourhood. It seemed as if he proposed to stop and take physical action. Although I was all ready for any trouble, poor Gillian was almost in tears with fright. In despair she shouted: 'Please go away and leave us alone!' I comforted her, with assurances that there was nothing to worry about: to ignore him. For thirty seconds he went on with his obscene insults until he shouted to Gillian: 'Be careful of him, lady, he's a wicked man!' Then with one last baleful glance at me, he drove off.

Gillian was speechless with shock for a few minutes. She fully recovered herself after we reached my home and she had a cup of strong coffee. She was so disillusioned. 'What is all the more disillusioning is that he seems to have proved some of your statements to be true,' she confessed dismally. The man simply couldn't appreciate that as I was entertaining her, I wasn't prepared to stop and enter into a long argument on race with him in the street. And so he had to react like an animal. Gillian appreciated that he may well have hated my TV remarks, 'but to scream like that in the street was really so stupid and senseless. He should have known better. And he sounded a very educated man.' What amazed her also was his apparent ignorance. On TV I didn't say blacks shouldn't date white girls, as he suggested I did. My statement had been that black men brutalised white girls. So goodness knows where he got his ideas from.

That wasn't an isolated case where blacks disillusioned Gillian. On another occasion we had come out of New Cross railway station. As we walked along the pavement of the traffic-congested street, two black girls in their late teens ran across the pedestrian crossing behind us, pointing and roaring abuse at me. 'You fucking sonofabitch! You go on television and disgrace black people. Look at him with a white girl.' They overtook us at a run, looking back and shouting, before disappearing into a shop. This time Gillian kept a cool head and paid no heed. We said little about the matter.

Not every black man hated my utterances on the box. A small number agreed with most of my statements, disagreeing with one or two points. Those were educated blacks, who felt the same way as I did about my fellow men in the world, who preferred to abstain from the company of blacks in London. They were happy I made my remarks, with the feeling that it was high time the black race was severely criticised. One of them gave me the impression that he almost died with joy on hearing my remarks. He confronted me one afternoon on the pavement outside W H Smith's, the bookshop, in West London's Notting Hill Gate. He was an elderly African, dressed in a smart lounge suit and hat. Tall and angular, his bloodshot eyes were sad and long-suffering and were set deep in a battered face. It was our first meeting, and I was expecting another hostile scene. But no. On discovering who I was, he snatched my hand and shook it vigorously. In a very jerky voice, he congratulated me profusely, adding that I didn't say enough on television. He was a wealthy landlord from West Africa's Sierra Leone, and had lived here twenty years. He owned several houses which, over the years, had—much to his regret—accommodated black people. Apparently, they caused endless damage, constantly raided the meters, and disappeared owing him a lot of rent. 'If you knew the amount of money they caused me to pay, my brother,' he complained. 'It was terrible. They left my houses like jungles. They kept blocking up the lavatories and sinks with all kinds of litter, and were actually urinating inside the kitchen sink.' For five minutes he poured out his troubles. He revealed that his tenants had been the cause of his suffering a nervous breakdown that resulted in long-term illness. 'Believe me, you hardly said a thing on television, my brother. There are many things you don't know that our people do here. What they've done to me, I will never forget.'

There were tears in his eyes as he spoke, and I did feel a stab of sympathy as I listened to his disturbing words. We parted with his pleading that I should continue to criticise publicly black people. I promised him I would if they continued their disgraceful ways.

Thus, one of the blacks who adored my television remarks. His words speak for themselves and could do without any opinions from me.

As it happened, my fellow men did continue to disgrace themselves. It seemed fate was determined that I shouldn't be given a chance to feel proud of them for a change. Apart from my own hostile encounters where they proved my claim on TV that they couldn't reason, they were involved in a number of serious incidents which proved most of my other statements, and which lowered my image of them to the lowest possible depth. And since my interview, life has been gloomy and frustrating because of my fellow men's behaviour. Of many examples I could give to illustrate their crimes, I must confine my examples to the few particular ones which have disturbed me most since they occurred: incidents that proved two important factors—that it was they who incurred white people's hatred, and that they were their own worst enemies. Beginning with the former, I've yet to get over my disgust after reading the headline-newspaper reports of a twenty-nine-year-old African's savagery in London. He stabbed his twenty-eight-year-old American girl-friend fourteen times in the arms and legs with a knife. And in court he volunteered the absurd but very convenient excuse that it was a tribal ritual. He confessed that he had been annoyed with his girl-friend for going off with friends at a time when he wanted her, and later slapped her mouth. But he insisted that his so-called tribal ritual wasn't done with malice or violence. His girl-friend denied this ritual farce and vowed he had stabbed her for no other reason than that she wasn't available when he wanted her. Though the press didn't try to put a racial interpretation on the matter, I knew that the attitude of the white masses reading the report would indeed be racial. As it happened, the matter was merely a newsflash and soon died down. But imagine the tumult there would have been had the assailant been white and the victim black. The press would have put the most powerful racial smell on the matter. The blacks would be foaming at the mouth. The Black Power magazines would have screamed insults at the white 'pigs', vowing that the blacks would retaliate. There would have been a public outcry. But so long as such an act is done behind a black face, all is well.

As it happened, I was well-acquainted with that African 'ritualist' and his girl-friend, the former particularly; who, until my TV appearances, had been a good pal. He was a broad-shouldered loud-mouth of muscular physique; well-educated, speaking with an assumed posh English accent. A few weeks after my interview, before the tribal ritual affair, he and his girl-friend for the first time met Betty at some black meeting, and later invited her to an African restaurant in the West End.

Betty was a tall, dark nineteen-year-old with a placid face, who showed a lot of interest in the Black Power struggle. The circumstances that brought about our meeting were dramatic. Arriving at the restaurant, she and the American girl went into the 'Ladies'. There Miss America gave Betty this important warning: 'One thing I had better warn you about black people is that they'll either want your money or they'll want to use violence on you.' Later, at the dining-table, Betty was introduced to a successful African author, who was well known for his violent Black Power activities in the past. A round-faced man in his mid-thirties with small wicked eyes that usually stare through dark glasses, expressionless as a crocodile's. Educated at an English university, he was a very passionate ideologist suffering from a 'chip' against white people, though it was obvious that he suffered more from conceit than he did from a chip. He and I, too, had fallen out over my TV interview. However, with complete lack of tact—as was typical of many blacks who came to eat there—he and his 'ritualist' friend preached loudly to Betty about race. It seemed that the writer might lose his temper with her any second as an argument developed between them. I sat with my uncle and a few other Africans at a nearby table, half-listening, quietly condemning blacks who preach on race in such an ill-chosen place as a restaurant. It was a late Saturday night, and good-time folks danced away to the sweet-blaring notes of an African band in the dance-hall at the end of the passage. At around midnight I emerged sweating from the packed dance-hall and briskly mounted the steps for some fresh air outside. As I reached the entrance door, I was in time to hear the writer shouting viciously: 'Now fuck off! And don't you ever dare come back to this centre again!' Several yards away, half-running into the night, was Betty, sobbing bitterly. I pushed past the writer and caught up with her. It wasn't my business, I admit, but I *knew* this was a case of unfair discrimination, and instinctively felt I should do something. I apologised for my sudden intrusion and asked if I could help. I introduced myself, consoled her and begged to be brought into the picture. The writer stood at the same place and watched us till we turned towards Leicester Square. Her sobbing subsided, and amid sniffs, she poured out the whole story. I assured her that the writer had no power whatsoever to eject her from the club or to stop visits by anybody. I insisted she come back and enjoy herself, with the guarantee that she'd be safe in my hands. But she refused, saying that she had experienced enough trouble for one night; and besides, it was time for her to go home anyway. We entered a cafe, ordered coffee. And for an hour she repeated everything in detail and talked of her interest in the Black Power struggle in England. Apparently the writer became furious any time she opposed any of his points as they ate. 'I-I-I just couldn't reason with him,' she stressed as she leaned her gaunt frame forward to drink coffee. 'He wouldn't listen to any of my views.'

She was independent of her parents, Betty, and lived alone in a bed-sitter. And that was why, she felt, the writer was keen to drive her home—because he knew she lived alone. So when she declined and insisted that she would go unaccompanied, he offered at least to see her off. Outside he became aggressive and rude 'and ordered me to start walking in that direction and keep walking'. He didn't assault her, 'but he threatened to, and I was so afraid that he would that I just started running.' It was at this point that she mentioned the warning of the American girl in the 'Ladies'.

It was a disturbing matter, and some days later when I visited the African restaurant for lunch, I told the Managing Secretary of the Club, whom I met on the stairs. She was an English lady in her late thirties with a very plain, bespectacled face; a lady whom many thought too weak and timid to be the boss of the Club. Politely, I said that many Africans were turning the restaurant into a meeting place for racial speeches, and this was in bad taste to some people. In an annoyingly defiant voice, she insisted, with a sort of helpless indifference, that she couldn't really do anything about it. 'All that would happen if we stopped them from coming here is that they'd run off to the press and say they're being victimised. And I'm not having it. So as far as I'm concerned that's a restaurant and anybody can go in there.' Appreciating her point, I informed her that: 'One of them, whom I'd rather keep anonymous, threatened a young white girl last Saturday night, and ordered her never to—'

'Oh, I know all about him!' she cut in loudly. 'He's done that to twenty-one other white girls here, myself included!'

That left me speechless. It was certainly new to me. On further enquiries for more details from other sources, I learnt that this writer used to threaten violence to white girls who refused him a dance, with the reminder that this was a black club; so they would do well to keep away. Apparently, many girls were so frightened that they never dared to come back again.

And remember, the two main characters involved in the stated incidents—the 'ritualist' and the writer—felt that I had no right to slur the blacks on television, condemning it as a wicked act of betrayal.

I think that out of all my encounters, what disgusted me most were the brutalities my fellow men carried out on themselves. I witnessed two horrible incidents, both taking place in full public view: the kind of incidents which would invite the typical sighing remark from some 'superior' white passer-by: 'There go those wretched blacks, killing each other again.' Walking along a tediously long road in Kent late one afternoon, my attention was drawn to heavy breathing behind me. I turned to face this fair-sized, bare-footed West Indian of about twenty-five. His bare feet slapped the ground as he increased his rapid steps. In his right hand was a long, thick cane. Someone, some-where had set fire to his temper. My heart missed a beat as, for one moment of shock, I thought he was after my neck. I was about to let fly with a powerful kick in self-defence, but just in time realised I was innocent. He overtook me. Thirty yards further on stood a group of young blacks. He approached one black teenage girl standing away from the group with her arms folded, an obstinate expression on her face. With sudden vicious strength, he lifted his arm and lashed the cane across this girl's face, following up with another blow across her body. The girl doubled up and let out the most horrible scream of pain that melted your bones to hear it. She wept bitterly as her assailant let fly with another brutal stroke on the back of her neck. There was pandemonium among the group. Black girls started to scream for the police, some weeping with fear and worry for the victim. The assailant accompanied his strokes with loud obscenities. Seeing what was happening, I ran up and tried to hold him back. He broke loose and went for the girl, giving her another blow on the face. I stepped between them and tried to beg him for mercy. The petrified girl clung on to my back for dear life.

'She's a wicked mother-fucker!' her assailant kept screaming. 'Me's going to fucking kill her!'

He kept circling, looking for a chance to land another blow without connecting with me. A crowd of blacks and whites had now gathered on both sides of the street. A few motorists slowed down to have a glimpse of the scene.

'Look, brother, leave her alone,' I pleaded, 'it's not worth it. You'll only hurt her.'

'Fuck off, man! She's a wicked girl. Me's going to lick the frigging hell out of her!'

At last, after a good three minutes more, two black men decided to come and help me. While they held him back, the girl's friends quickly escorted her into a house and the door was slammed shut. What the matter was all about, I didn't stop to find out, as I had to be punctual for an appointment. I simply felt that if such brutality really were necessary, it needn't have taken place in public. I overhead that it was a boy-friend, girl-friend dispute.

On another occasion, an excited crowd of blacks and whites were assembled at the gate of a shabby semi-detached house near a set of traffic lights in New Cross. An ambulance was there. Curiously, I joined the crowd. A gruesome spectacle met my eyes. A teenage black girl was seated on a stool, whimpering feebly, her face soaked with tears and blood. She seemed on the point of passing out. At her feet was a great puddle of blood, which had found its source from her bandaged neck and head where, barely twenty minutes before, she had been savagely stabbed by a black landlord. Sympathetic black girls held and comforted her till she was gently transferred to an ambulance wheel-chair and carried into the vehicle. It was at that moment that the police arrived. Three Panda cars turned up almost simultaneously, and the officers observed the poor girl before allowing the ambulance to leave. They entered the adjoining house to arrest the landlord, a thick-set man around thirty years of age with short, close-cut hair. At least he went quietly—unlike most blacks. A wave of silence engulfed the crowd as he was put into a police car and driven away. The police also took possession of the knife he used.

A shocked elderly black who lived in the house breathlessly poured out the details to the crowd. The girl owed three months' rent and had been given notice by the landlord to leave. But she had been unable to find accommodation. For those three months life had been nothing short of hell for her. She suffered constant harassment from the landlord, who saw fit to burst into her room and threaten her with violence. The old witness swore that on one occasion he overheard the landlord warn her: 'I promise you I'll kill you if you don't leave this house.' His temper eventually overtook him and kill her he almost did. No doubt the law gave him his just reward.

So there it is. You can see now the sort of treatment that blacks subject their own people to: treatment that makes the practices of white racialists against them seem so blessedly insignificant. Truly, for me to say that my fellow men behave like animals would be an abuse to the animal kingdom, because even animals themselves display a more innate sense of decorum.

I've said all I can about the black man in England. Their duty now is to elevate their own sense of values and return home. As other ethnic groups in the world have done, they should build up and develop their own motherlands; try to rectify their own evils and shortcomings; learn to plan in the long-term, and above all, learn to live together like human beings. Until they can do for themselves what the other races in the world have done for themselves, never will they be respected or regarded as human beings equal with the whites. There's no gold to be found on the streets of Britain, only degradation. And if my fellow men are content to remain here, carrying on with their present behaviour, they're merely fulfilling the belief voiced by many white people like the famous author Charles Carrol: 'The Negro is a beast, but created with articulate speech, and hands, that he may be of service to his master—the White man.'

So now we ask: Will the black man in England—in the world even—get a hold over himself? Will he come to appreciate the importance of having a brain? Will he abandon his present ways and turn over a new life? Are we to be yet surprised? We can only wait and watch. It's entirely up to the black man now. At the moment his future seems dark and sombre. And only he can change it.

4